The Committed Organisation

To: Mathew, Andrew & Kathryn

The Committed Organisation

How to develop companies to compete successfully in the 1990s

Graham Saunders

Gower

Published by
Gower Publishing Company Limited,
Gower House,
Croft Road,
Aldershot,
Hants GU11 3HR,
England
Printed in Great Britain by Dotesios (Printers) Ltd.
Bradford-on-Avon, Wiltshire.

British Library Cataloguing in Publication Data

Saunders, Graham
The committed organisation.
1. Organizational change
2. Industrial management
I. Title
658.4'06 HD58.8

ISBN 0-566-02493-4

Contents

Preface vii

Acknowledgements xi

PART ONE: DEVELOPING THE VISION

Overview 3

1 The nature of organisations 5
Organisations as adjusting to their environments–Organisation culture: a model–Organisation culture and organisation change–Summary and conclusions

2 Commitment and involvement 16

3 The Japanese manufacturing process: what can we learn from it? 20
Japanese manufacturing system–Japanese approach to managing people–Japanese and teamwork–Quality Circles–Summary and conclusions

PART TWO: THE ORGANISATION DEVELOPMENT PROCESS

Overview 43

4 Organisation design and the committed culture 47
Hierarchy–Integrating the functions–Summary and conclusions

5 The workshop approach to organisation development 56
The planning workshop–Workshop principles–The role of the headman–Summary and conclusions

6 **Developing the guidelines** 78
The workshop programme—Workshop outcome—Summary and conclusions

7 **The cascading workshop programme** 84
Supervisor workshops—A workshop for specialist support staff—Operator workshops

8 **Workshops to facilitate change** 98
Organisation audit—Building intergroup cooperation—Building boss-team relationships

9 **Union workshop** 109
Union relations: conflict or cooperation—The union representative: does he bleed?—The management-union workshop—Action following the workshop—Summary and conclusions

10 **Team structures** 126
Building manufacturing teams—Incorporating matrix principles—Supervisors as team leaders—Summary and conclusions

11 **Communications** 140
Communication systems—Why so many organisations communicate badly—Improving communications in company X—Principles of effective communications—Summary and conclusions

12 **Support for the organisation development process** 154
The organisation development consultant—Training

13 **Personnel systems and personnel departments** 160

14 **Conclusions** 165

APPENDICES

1 **Management planning workshop** 169
2 **Management principles workshop** 175
3 **Supervisor workshop** 179
4 **Specialist workshop** 184
5 **Monthly briefing groups** 188
6 **Management-union workshops** 192

Reading list 196

Index 203

Preface

This book has been written for people who spend their working day managing (at whatever level) in large organisations. It has also been written for people who teach, train or otherwise develop the skills of these practical managers. But above all, it has been written for the people who lead and direct our large organisations.

This book is about the development of more effective organisations, and in any organisation development programme it is top management who must provide the vision, who must develop the understanding and commitment, and who must direct, inspire, cajole, and bully the people with the day-to-day responsibility for making things happen.

This book has been written in the belief that many organisations have not been able to make full use of the knowledge, skills and energy of their employees, and have failed to develop their people's potential. Many organisations have become inflexible, unable to react to changes in the environment in which they operate. What is proposed is a development programme that can be used to increase productivity and flexibility. This organisation development programme involves two stages:

1 The development by the top management of a 'vision' of what the organisation should be like in the future if it is to:
   (*a*) overcome the problems it is currently facing;
   (*b*) adjust to the changes that are taking place in the environment;
   (*c*) make fuller use of the potential to contribute of the organisation's members i.e. its employees.

   This vision will have political, economic, social and technical dimensions.

2 The translation of the vision into an action plan for change. This action plan should:
   (*a*) incorporate our increasing knowledge of motivation and the behaviour of individuals in organisations;
   (*b*) be sufficiently flexible to allow the management within each part of the organisation to interpret the organisation's vision in the light of their own particular problems, needs and objectives;
   (*c*) begin with change at the top and 'cascade down';
   (*d*) involve all members of the organisation at all levels, but each at the right time;
   (*e*) provide feedback and a review of progress to ensure that implementation of the plan is systematic and controlled.

To reflect the two stage nature of the organisation development programme, this book is divided into two parts. Part One explores ways in which an organisation 'vision' can be developed, looks at the nature of organisations and how cultures can be changed, and examines the ways the Japanese manage. Part One deals with where we should be going and why. Part Two offers a detailed step-by-step strategy of how to translate this vision into practical action.

There are three reasons for believing that the action recommended in this book will enable organisations to make substantial improvements in their competitive positions.

1 There have been important advances from the applied behaviour success during the last two decades that have increased our knowledge of the way organisations work, and how they can be made more competitive.
2 There is an example of a nation that has successfully applied this knowledge. That nation is Japan. They have taken the ideas developed, (though not adopted) in the West, and over many years learned how to adapt them to their own culture. Japan has always been good at plagiarising Western ideas. It is time we learned from the Japanese how we can improve the effectiveness of our organisations.
3 Practical experience of consulting in organisations throughout the world has convinced the author that these ideas work in practice. There are many 'ifs and buts' and these will be discussed in the book, but given the drive, vision and commitment at the top, we can transform our organisations. Some are already well on the way.

Throughout this book the words he, him, himself appear, but the words she, her and herself do not. It is not intended to appear sexist;

there are many women taking key roles in the development of organisations. Our language has not as yet reacted to sexual equality by developing words that mean 'he or she' or 'his or her'. In the interest of brevity and style, please assume the he always means 'he or she', his always means 'his or her' and himself always means 'herself or himself'.

Graham Saunders

Acknowledgements

The ideas in this book come from many sources. The writings and research of academics have laid a theoretical foundation. Some of these influences have been acknowledged in the text, but in addition, I wish to express my thanks to Toby Wall and Chris Clegg of the SSRC/MRC Applied Psychology Research Unit at Sheffield University and to Joel Richman of Manchester Polytechnic for their counsel and support over many years. Most of the ideas, however, have their origin in the knowledge and wisdom of the many executives and managers with whom I have worked helping to bring about change in large organisations. I would particularly like to acknowledge a conceptual debt to Jim Henderson, President of the Cummins Engine Company, who has demonstrated not only the capacity to develop a clear vision for the future, but has also shown how to translate that vision into action to more fully utilise the talents of the people at all levels, and to produce a flexible and committed culture.

If this book has merit, it is largely due to the ideas of these people. I have attempted to translate their experience, knowledge and wisdom into a practical programme for managing change in large organisations. The failings of the book are mine alone.

Finally, my special thanks to Dawn Feany, Anne Eglin, Philip Scott and Les Young for checking and typing the manuscript, and for their support, encouragement, and creative criticism.

Acknowledgements

PART ONE
DEVELOPING THE VISION

Overview

In a recent best selling book entitled *Theory Z; How American Business can meet the Japanese challenge*, W. G. Ouchi argues that top management must accept responsibility for managing change and improving organisation effectiveness. To Ouchi the first stage in this process is the establishment of a corporate 'vision' of the future. Top management must develop a clear picture of the organisation they want to achieve. Once they have established this vision the next stage is to plan a programme of action to transform the organisation from what it is now, to what is desired in the future. To Ouchi changes towards a more effective and competitive organisation will primarily come through better use of the human resources. Therefore, the vision should be mostly concerned with a philosophy of how people should be managed. Top management should consider their approach to management style, to work ethic, the environment at work, teamwork, fairness and incentives.

This book takes a similar position. Significant improvements in the competitive position of any large organisation can only come from making much more effective use of their human resources. As all organisations will have equal access to advancing technology, the more successful will be those able to motivate the people to make fullest use of this technology. More effective use of human resources will only come from the vision and leadership of the people at the top, and their capacity to manage a major development process to bring about changes in organisation culture.

Part One of this book is designed to assist managers in their task of developing this vision: a clear understanding of the efficient, flexible and competitive organisation culture, towards which they should be moving. Chapter One reviews the nature of organisations and emphasises the importance of developing the capacity to react rapidly and flexibly to changes in the commercial, economic, technical, political and social environment in which they operate. Chapter Two, discusses the nature of commitment and argues that the competitive organisation is one that has achieved high levels of commitment to the organisation's goals from employees at all levels. These two chapters bring together the key concepts on which this book is based; that successful organisations must achieve both a committed membership, and the flexibility to adapt to a changing environment.

Chapter Three reviews the way the Japanese manage their organisations and particularly what the Japanese do to achieve commitment, efficiency and flexibility. The main emphasis of this chapter is on how the Japanese maximise the contributions of all their people. Ouchi also looked at the Japanese way of managing, and Chapter Three summarises his interpretation of the reasons for the Japanese success.

It is hoped that Part One will increase the appreciation by the management within organisations that cultures can be changed. It is also hoped that the models and ideas presented in Part One will help managers to develop their own thinking about the way their human resources should be managed. When this vision is developed it can be used as the foundation for an organisation development programme. How to manage the organisation development programme and achieve the vision is described in Part Two.

1 The Nature of Organisations

There are not many 'organisation theory' jokes; the subject does not naturally lend itself to humour. Probably the best known concerns three men sitting in a bar discussing the different management styles in their organisation. The first is from a large oil company. He explains that what really matters in the oil business is to get the investment policy right, so top management receive large quantities of commercial and geological data. They review this data and make decisions about where to invest. Information flows up, decisions are made at the top and implemented below. The second man shakes his head and says that his organisation does not work like that at all. He works for a computer company. Change is so rapid, and the technology so complex that top management could never have enough information to make decisions. They identify trends, appoint project teams of specialists to investigate commercial opportunities and make recommendations. These recommendations are invariably accepted because the team members, rather than top management, have the expertise. The skill of top management lies in identifying and developing talented people to man the teams. The third companion scratches his head. His organisation is very different; they use the mushroom method of management. In the mushroom method, people are kept in the dark for days on end. Occasionally the door is opened by top management having a look to see how the people are developing. 'At last', the people say, 'I can see some light!' Then top management shovel manure on top of them and close the door for a few more days.

This joke illustrates one thing about organisations: they vary. Even commercial organisations vary enormously one from another, and if we compare commercial with government, educational, charity or social organisations, the differences between them in terms of structure and culture are even greater.

Most members of organisations take for granted the rules and values that govern their organisation. They may grumble about the boss not listening, or relationships with marketing, or the unfair job evaluation system, and they may argue for change, but they do not think of the origins of the differences between their culture and those in other organisations. If they do speculate in these areas, they will tend to think of the culture as being the product of the influence of powerful leaders in the past.

The fact that these differences exist is brought home when people move from one organisation to another. In their old job, they knew how things worked, and the rules you had to follow if you were to progress and to avoid trouble. In the new organisation these rules are different. What seemed entirely appropriate in their old organisation is not 'the done thing' in the new one. The differences will be particularly difficult to come to terms with, if the two organisations are very different in size, objectives, geographical dispersion, ownership, technology, or competitive environment. To adjust to this different environment the newcomer must rapidly forget the old lessons and values and learn the new.

Examples of the enormous diversity between different organisations can be found in all aspects of organisation life. One of the best examples lies in the way different organisations approach establishing the level of salary of their members. In the civil service and education the employee's salary depends upon his grade and his seniority. In most small, entrepreneurial marketing-orientated organisations, the employee's salary will be based on a decision made by his boss, who attempts to match salary increase to his judgement of the performance of the individual. In large commercial organisations there will usually be a compromise, a cost of living increase with a small part of any annual adjustment allocated following an assessment of merit. If you ask top management in each of these three organisations what they believe about the relationship between money and performance, you will invariably get very different responses. The entrepreneur will be quite convinced that money is a motivator, the civil servant will see the salary paid to an individual as part of a contract – the employee provides his time and talent in return for agreed rewards, the big organisation man will believe that there should be a motivational aspect to salary but that because it is difficult to be fair and consistent this should only represent a small part of the total package.

Behaviour and attitudes towards rewards is only one of the many subtle variations to be found between different types of organisations. Major differences will also be found in the way communications are managed, the way disputes are settled, in the amount of group decision making, in the rules for dress, in the way people are addressed, in the power of the management, and so on. This chapter is about how to make sense of the tremendous variety of attitudes, values and behaviours that characterise the many organisations found in our society. We must understand the nature of our organisation, before we can determine the action needed to improve its effectiveness. Otherwise we shall prescribe the wrong treatment.

Organisations as adjusting to their environments

Until the 1960s most of the research and writings on organisations was characterised by a search for the 'one best way'. This might be the best way to structure, or the best way to design a reward system, or the best way to communicate. This approach was never very fruitful. The rules that operated in one organisation did not seem to work at all effectively in others. These negative findings led researchers to approach the problem in a rather different way. In an influential and now famous book *Organisation and Environment* published in 1967 Lawrence and Lorsch reported their findings on investigations into different organisations. They looked at successful and unsuccessful organisations in three industries; plastics, containers and food. They looked at the way each organised the marketing function, how each managed change, also the different approaches to the management of people, and the degree of formality of structure. They found that they could detect organisational differences between the more successful and less successful plastics companies. They also found significant differences between more and less successful companies in container manufacture, and more and less successful companies in the food industry. What they did not find was a pattern of success for all companies. The successful plastics company was different from the successful food company. Some of the characteristics of successful food companies were present in unsuccessful container companies.

They concluded that what matters is not the existence of management style 'A', or organisation structure 'B', but that the organisation characteristics of the company fit into the environment in which it is operating. The successful companies took on characteristics which allowed them to take advantage of opportunities in the environment, and also manage any threats. If the environment changed, then the successful organisation changed to complement it. Probably the best analogy to illustrate their main point can be taken from ecology – the study of living organisms and their adjustment to their environment. This analogy has been used extensively by people interested in understanding organisations and promoting organisational change.

An amoeba lives in an aquatic environment. It survives by taking 'inputs' from its environment (microscopic plants) and transforming them into elements it can use (energy, body-tissue) to allow it to grow and survive. The amoeba also continually searches for the most advantageous environment – where the food is plentiful, the temperature ideal, the pollution minimal, predators absent. The successful amoeba is one which uses for its own ends what is available, and continuously searches for a more advantageous environment.

An organisation can be seen in the same way. It takes inputs from its environment, and transforms these inputs into something it can use to allow it to survive and prosper – an output. If the environment changes, it must also change in order to ensure its own long term survival.

A manufacturing company takes raw material (input), machines and assembles that raw material (transformation), and sells the product to the customer (outputs). If the company makes engines for the automotive industry, and the price of diesel fuel drops compared with the price of petrol, then the organisation must change all three elements (inputs, transformations, outputs) to take account of the changed market demands if it is to remain viable and competitive. All types of organisations can be analysed using this model. For instance, a restaurant also has inputs (food) transformation (cooking) and outputs (meals). It must also adjust its activities to a changing environment (e.g. increased wealth of its customers, new environmental health regulations) if it is to survive and prosper.

This model, known as an open-systems model, has proved to be a valuable way of approaching the study of organisations. It gets away from the idea that there is one ideal way of designing or structuring an organisation, or managing a sales force, or communicating. The open systems approach takes as its starting point that different organisations have different inputs and outputs. There is no one 'best way'; only the best way for each organisation at any point in time.

An open-systems analysis is a useful exercise for organisation members who are taking on responsibility for contributing towards their own organisation's development because:

1 It helps people to see their own organisation as a potentially flexible and dynamic system;

2 It helps people to understand their own culture, and how and why it developed;
3 It helps the development of a vision of the alternative cultures that can be developed within each organisation;
4 It allows the evaluation of the relevance of these alternatives for the achievement of greater organisation effectiveness.

Readers who wish to know more about the open-system approach are referred to the reading list at the end of the book.

The following section describes a model that interprets the variations in culture found between different organisations.

Organisation culture: a model

In 1976 Charles Handy published his book *Understanding Organisations.* Chapter 7 of this book presents a description of four different types of organisation cultures, and proposes ways in which each type can be measured. Culture is a concept that is difficult to tie down or be precise about. Handy's approach helps people to understand the concept better, and also to gain insights into their own organisations. This section summarises Handy's main points and suggests ways in which the concepts can be used to facilitate change.

Handy believes that organisations can be categorised into four cultures. Large organisations may operate with different cultures in different departments or units. All organisational units will contain elements of more than one culture, but one of the four cultures: 'power', 'role', 'task' and 'person' will be the dominant culture.

Power

The chief characteristic of a power culture is the existence at the organisation's centre of a powerful and dominant leader whose will and influence pervade all decision making. Influence is exercised through key individuals, close to and trusted by the central power source, and who understand and are able to anticipate the wishes of the leader. There are few rules and procedures, few committees to convene or reports to be deliberated over. Decision making is rapid and based on snap, 'seat-of-the-pants', reactions. Power organisations can move rapidly, grasp opportunities and react to threat or danger. They depend upon the person at the centre, and upon the quality of his judgement. Growth is a problem, because with increased size the centre will become less able to control and integrate. Power cultures are uncomfortable to work in if you have not established links with the power base.

New, rapid growth, entrepreneurial organisations often have power cultures, but so do some trade unions. In large commercial organisations marketing is more likely to have power characteristics than manufacturing or production.

Role

Role culture is the main characteristic of the 'steady state' organisation, where the problems are to integrate a variety of different tasks so that the overall organisational objectives are met. The tasks are completed by teams of functional specialists working in sub-organisations e.g. purchasing, marketing, personnel, finance and work is integrated by the top management (the board in a commercial organisation). Each member of the organisation has his own task to perform; if all the members perform adequately, as laid down by procedures, the ultimate results will be as planned. Role cultures move carefully and take minimum risks. Decisions are made by committees, procedures (for handling disputes, for defining tasks, etc.) are well developed, and individual creativity and initiative are potentially disruptive.

The role organisation will succeed as long as it operates in a stable environment. When next year is like this year, the outcome will be good. When the organisation can control its environment, when the market is stable and predictable, or where the product life is a long one, then rules and procedures and programmed work will be successful. But role cultures are slow to perceive the need for change and slow to change even if the need is seen. If the market, or the competitive environment changes, the role culture will forge straight ahead, like a super-tanker that sees on its radar rocks five miles ahead but is unable to change course in time to avoid them. Recent history has provided too many examples of organisations that were unable to adjust in time. Any transition towards viability (adjustment to the environment) has usually been accompanied by a change in culture. A decrease in role culture and an increase in power culture has often been necessary to ensure the rapid and far reaching changes required. Large organisations going through painful adjustment programmes, also frequently report an increase in 'task culture'.

Task

The whole emphasis of the task culture is on getting things done. The approach is to bring together the appropriate resources and the right people and let them get on with it. It is a team culture, where heirarchy is minimal, and people are evaluated on the basis of their ability to contribute to the team's success. In large organisations, R & D will often have many characteristics of a task culture and it will often be the appropriate culture for project teams put together to deal with a specific problem. Small professional practices (doctors, management consultants, architects, solicitors) will often operate as teams as will many non-commercial organisations; drama groups, local political organisations. Task cultures are flexible and sensitive, able to react swiftly and to use the creative talents of all the members effectively. But they can be difficult to direct and control and expensive in their use of resources. They are not appropriate where routines and stability are needed. They are fun to work in, and are the culture most in tune with current ideologies of change and adaptation, individual freedom and low status differentials. However, that does not necessarily make them the right culture to have.

Person

The fourth culture is not usually found in commercial organisations, but can be identified in many academic establishments, as well as hippy communes and kibbutzim. The essential feature of the person organisation is that it exists for the benefit of its members rather than to produce an output of goods or services. They are cultures in which the members 'do their own things'. Structure and control are minimal. The stereotype is the university lecturer who does the minimum teaching needed to retain his position (required by the rules as laid down by the 'role' part of his organisation) so that he has the time and resources to build his own career and pursue his own research interests. The organisation is his base, but he has little concern for involvement in activities that are directed towards achieving its overall objectives. Specialists in organisations – computer people, hospital consultants – sometimes behave as if they are in a 'person' culture.

As part of this model Handy speculates on the origins of different organisation cultures. What are the reasons why some organisations develop the bureaucratic characteristics of a role culture, whilst others seem to remain dominated by a key individual at the helm? He suggests there are seven types of influence at work:

1 *Age*: New organisations tend to be either aggressive and independent (power) or flexible and adaptable (task) or a combination of the two. As they mature they tend to stabilise and develop more formal structures, more careful decision making, and more rules and regulations (role).
2 *Ownership*: Organisations which are still run by their founder-owners tend to be power cultures. Large multinationals tend to expect large quantities of information to be sent to head office from their satellite organisations and are reassured by the

presence of developed systems and procedures. Their subordinate plants tend towards role cultures to meet the expectations of head office.

3 *Size*: Size is probably the most important influence. Large organisations tend to be more formal and therefore have role cultures although they may contain sub-organisations that are task or power. As a power culture gets larger the central power can no longer hold it together. Teams cannot maintain group cohesion if they contain more than about a dozen people. Size pushes organisations towards role cultures, away from task or power.

4 *Technology*: Organisations that have invested heavily in technology tend toward role cultures. The cost of breakdown is high, so close monitoring and depth of expertise are necessary. If the manufacturing process involves 30 operations from raw material to finished part and an error in any one would scrap the piece, the organisation will not encourage innovation and experimentation. Mass production leads to formalised procedures.

5 *Goals*: The objectives of an enterprise are seldom as clear cut as they seem. Most commercial organisations do not behave as if their goal is to maximise profit; their goal appears to be to make things or provide a service, and hopefully to do this profitably. Hospitals, schools, and local authorities could see their goals as service to the community, or maintenance of standards. Other organisation goals could be to survive, increase market share, grow, look after employee's welfare, provide enjoyable work experiences, improve the corporate reputation, increase the value of shares, provide the chairman with a knighthood, and so on. Growth goals are more appropriate to a power or task culture, (although role organisations often achieve growth), employee welfare goals are more appropriate to task and person cultures. Reliability and prestige go with role cultures. Power cultures take pride in their results, role cultures in their products.

6 *The environment*: The more rapidly the environment changes, the greater the need for the organisation to be reactive, and the less will a role culture be appropriate. Environmental change could take many forms – economic (depressed demand), competition (the Japanese are going to enter our market), market trends (from medium to low tar cigarettes), social values, (hostility towards pollution). As the environment changes the effective organisations have the capacity to understand the changes taking place, to take the necessary action to

adjust to them. Conversely, the well adjusted organisation in a stable environment, needs to avoid making changes for change's sake. The hospital boards are often accused of being too prone to major reorganisations when the task they perform and their goals are essentially unchanged over fairly long periods of time. Task and power cultures react well to changes in the environment, role cultures are slow to see the need for change, and slow to change even when the need is recognised.

7 *People*: The key people in an organisation have a great deal of influence over the culture that develops. The new personnel manager who insists on job evaluation and a procedure manual will be moving the organisation towards a role culture. A charismatic leader may be able to maintain a power culture despite increases in the size and complexity of his organisation.

In the next section, the importance of this model for understanding how organisations can effectively adjust to the environment in which they operate is discussed.

Organisation culture and organisation change

Handy's model is concerned with describing the nature and origins of different organisation cultures. He is not concerned with changing organisations, although he does suggest that change is easier to bring about in power and task cultures than it is in role or person cultures. Nevertheless his ideas are important because they help us understand the organisations in which we work and how they can be made more effective.

The role culture describes the organisations in which most of us work. If we are teachers or civil servants, if we work for any of the large manufacturing organisations, or a local authority we will be working for an organisation whose predominant culture is 'role', although there will probably be some elements of power, task and person cultures. The success of role cultures is critical to the success of any advanced industrial nation. Commercial organisations must be profitable, hospitals and schools must provide an effective and relevant service, our government must be able to make just decisions if an industrialised society is to thrive. To successfully achieve its goals the organisation must be aware of the opportunities available to it, and the problems it faces, so that the opportunities are grasped and the problems overcome. It must be sensitive to its environment and able to change as the environment changes. But one of the characteristics of role organisations is their poor ability to make adjustments to changes in their environment.

In Handy's words 'Role cultures are slow to perceive the need for change, and slow to change even if the need is seen'.

In Part Two we will be developing ideas about how we can build the capacity to change into role organisations. If the organisation has the capacity for change it has a choice, whether to carry on doing the same tasks in the same way on the one hand, or whether to choose new tasks, new goals or new approaches on the other. The successful organisation should look to stability if its own environment is stable and predictable. But it should scan the environment for signs that the future is bringing different challenges than those the organisation has been managing in the past, and it should be capable of reacting to those challenges.

The 1970s and 1980s have brought increasing speed of change in the environment in which our role organisations function. Probably the major changes with which they have had to come to terms are:

1 Increasing competition from Japan and the Far East;
2 Increases in energy cost;
3 Enormous strides in information technology;
4 Growing concerns with environmental protection;
5 Economic recession;
6 Growing concerns with occupational health hazards;
7 Restrictions in government spending;
8 International protectionism.

Few organisations in any sphere of activity have been free from the influences of changes of this sort. Some have adjusted well and emerged stronger and more prosperous. Others have not survived, or survived only with government aid.

Have these organisations been trapped in an environment suddenly and unpredictably turned hostile? Or did they fail to see the trends? Or did they see the trends, but fail to take any action to manage through them? If some prospered and some failed, then it would appear that the failures were unable to adjust to a changing environment. In particular, the larger Japanese organisations seem to have weathered the economic storms of the last decade and emerged with increased prosperity and an increased market share. The Japanese seem to have achieved, to a much larger extent than their European and American competitors, the capacity to manage large 'role' organisations in a way that allows them to continuously and effectively adjust to changes in the environment in which they operate. How they have achieved this will be discussed in Chapter Three.

Summary and conclusions

The main points made in this chapter can be summarised as follows:

1 Organisations vary widely in many ways: for instance the rules they operate, their values, goals, management styles. These differences can be referred to as differences in culture.
2 There is no one culture that would be relevant for all organisations. The successful organisation is one which can adapt its culture to its environment.
3 Handy presents a useful typology of cultures: power, task, role, and person. Most employees work in role cultures.
4 One of the characteristics of the role culture is its stability. The role culture does not find it easy to adjust itself to a rapidly changing environment.
5 The environment in which many organisations operate has been changing more rapidly during the last decade, and many role organisations in Europe and North America have failed to adjust effectively to this increased tempo.
6 The Japanese organisations have been able to make these adjustments. They seem to have developed organisations with the ability to utilise the talents of all their members to identify and grasp opportunities, and to identify and overcome problems.

In order to manage change, organisation members need to understand their own organisation's culture, and to see their own organisation as a potentially flexible and dynamic system. Only then can they develop a vision of the future and an appreciation of the route they need to take to achieve that vision.

2 Commitment and Involvement

Participation has been a vogue word since the mid-1970s. At that time the appointment of 'workers' representatives' to the top-level decision making boards of major business, educational, and government organisations was being advocated in many European countries. Except in Scandinavia these appointments of 'worker directors' did not receive enough political support to overcome the hostility of many sections of the business world, and never became widespread. But increasingly as the decade progressed the talk turned from participation through representation toward more direct forms of participation, to designing and managing organisations in a way that encouraged more say by its members at all levels in those activities which directly affected them, and over which they could have some influence.

Surveys were published showing that there was demand at all levels in organisations for better information channels, more explanations on what is happening and why, more regular meetings with management, and the opportunity for people to be consulted and put their views. The same surveys showed little demand for worker directors, or for the opportunity to get a bigger say in management decisions on finance or investment. One of these surveys is discussed in more detail in Chapter Eleven.

This increasing interest in direct participation during the 1970s led to a great deal of action, mostly experimental, in many organisations. Jobs have been designed in new ways following consultation with employees, systems of consultation with organisation members at all levels have been established. There are now a number of books which describe these projects in participation and provide evidence for their success (some are listed at the end of this book). The evidence is growing that there are a number of advantages to a participatory approach to the management of human resources. The advocates of greater participation in the management of organisations argue that it brings the following advantages:

1 Feelings of commitment to an organisation's aims are developed when people are given the opportunity to have some influence over what happened. Conversely they feel powerless when they are not allowed to influence events, and lose feelings of commitment.
2 More involvement and participation increase the member's understanding of the organisation's aims and objectives, and this understanding develops a greater appreciation of the common interest and mutual inter-dependence of all sections of the enterprise: management, shopfloor, shareholders or owners, union representatives, suppliers, customers and consumers. Participation will therefore lead to an improved industrial relations climate and a more cooperative workforce; less us *v* them.
3 People, particularly but not only, at the lower levels of organisations, are often capable of contributing much more than is normally asked of them. The skills, knowledge and interests of employees at all levels can only be fully tapped if they have the opportunity to contribute through some form of participation.
4 Participation will bring about greater job satisfaction and well-being and therefore not only bring benefits to the employee but also indirect benefits to the organisation through lower labour turnover and lower absenteeism.
5 An interest in participation can help the image of the organisation by indicating a concern for the workforce and a sense of social responsibility towards them.
6 Social and educational trends have decreased the willingness of employees to be managed in an authoritarian way. Employees who are not involved become alienated. This means that it is now more than ever true that effective management is only possible with the consent of the managed, which necessitates their involvement.

There are, however, disadvantages in using a participatory approach, the chief of which is that it is time consuming. Consulting with subordinates takes management time, that could be used for other things. Delegating responsibility for decision making to work teams leads to their spending time at meetings when they could be working on production. There has to be a belief on the part of the management that this utilisation of their own and their people's time is worthwhile. They must believe that time spent in ensuring acceptance of decisions will be paid back with dividends through time saved in implementing decisions. They must believe that work teams will be more effective at their jobs because of the problem solving, integration, and increased motivation generated at the meetings.

A second potential disadvantage is that power is delegated to a lower level in the organisation, where wisdom may not also always be located. The senior people may have the long term insight and the experience to make better decisions, but they have given away the power of their position. Again, the disadvantage in a culture that has achieved high levels of member involvement will be more apparent than real. The work group will rapidly develop their own wisdom and expertise, and the wise counsellor will make his influence felt because he will be seen as expert and able to help the group attain their objectives.

There is a strong case, therefore, for advocating an approach to the management of organisations that increase the involvement of the people at all levels. By doing so we develop the knowledge skills and commitment of organisation members. However, because of the disadvantages, there are situations when the use of a participatory management style would be counter-productive.

1 When decisions have to be made quickly, and there is no time for a consultation programme. If, in a soccer game, a striker is provided with a perfectly weighted through ball into the penalty area, his team-mates do not want him to consult on whether he should shoot to the left hand or to the right hand side of the goal. They will expect him to make an authoritarian and autonomous decision. Members of organisations readily accept that some decisions must be made rapidly and, if trust is present, they will accept the decision, even if they do not agree with it.
2 When decisions are trivial. Being consulted on matters you consider of little importance becomes a bore.
3 When subordinates do not have the information or knowledge to make a sound decision. People will accept that there are areas where they do not have the knowledge to make a sound decision. If trust is present they will accept that these decisions should be left to the people with the relevant expertise. They may ask for training so that they understand the problem better and so that they will be able to contribute in the future to decisions which affect them.
4 When there is conflict between the needs of the members and the needs of the organisation. No one expects to be given a free

rein to set their own salary levels. There will be situations where a manager finds that his subordinates will not support a course of action he believes to be imperative. Such a situation is described in the case history in Part Two. In this situation the plant manager imposed an unpopular decision, but invited participation in its implementation. There are penalties in imposing decisions in terms of lowered commitment and decreased trust, but there are situations where the price must be paid.

A participatory approach therefore is not recommended in all situations. The changes that have revolutionised a number of organisations in the late 1970s and early 1980s, could not have taken place in a participatory atmosphere. There was not enough time, and given the necessity for a rapid and ruthless reduction in the numbers of the organisation's members, there was clearly conflict between the short-term needs of the organisation and the needs of the organisation's members. Major and rapid organisational surgery requires the use of position power operated in an authoritarian way.

Summary and conclusions

Participation therefore has its advantages and also has its disadvantages. It can increase commitment, contribution, understanding, productivity and flexibility. On the other hand it can be expensive and time consuming and it certainly is not always appropriate. But the organisation that is intent on building a committed culture must move towards a participatory style that emphasises involvement of the people.

A recurrent theme in this book is that Western organisations need to take action to develop a culture where all employees are able to, and wish to become involved in and influence their own working environment. This involvement will bring coordinated action to identify and solve the problems, grasp the opportunities and ensure an ongoing adjustment to any changes in the environment.

In the next chapter, the way the Japanese achieve this commitment from their people, through consistently following policies of involvement, is discussed. Many of the large Japanese organisations provide living examples of how large 'role' type organisations use all their members' talents to ensure the long-term prosperity of the organisation.

3 The Japanese Manufacturing Process: What can we learn from it?

In the mid 1960s the Japanese had virtually no car industry. In 1982 their production capacity was equal to the USA and greater than Western Europe. Virtually all the world growth in car sales in the 1970s went to Japan. Their impact had been particularly pervasive in the USA. Imports of cars rose from 200,000 to 2,200,000 between 1969 and 1980. During the same period the Japanese sales of small trucks rose from 33,000 units to 600,000 units. The impact of the Japanese intrusion into their markets on the native American manufacturers has been far reaching. By the early eighties all the large American motor manufacturers were making losses and 250,000 car workers had lost their jobs.

The impact of the Japanese on the motor industry in Europe has not been as great as in America. This is largely because of the European's ability to protect their home markets by erecting tariffs or by coming to agreements on import quotas with the Japanese. But in both Europe and North America the Japanese have been able to make major inroads in a variety of consumer goods other than cars; noticeably television sets, stereo equipment, cameras, and motor cycles. In some cases the effect of this competition has been to destroy the home industry.

The Japanese growth as an exporting nation has been complemented by the growth of vast, diversified organisations within Japan. In 1978 Mitsubishi had a turnover of $106 billion. Each of the top five Japanese companies outsold both General Motors and Shell during that year. Beside these companies, ICI is a midget. An average growth rate during the 1970s of 4. 5 per cent (USA 3.3 per cent, UK 1.8 per cent) has led to the personal consumption of goods and services of the Japanese being higher than that of the British, and quickly approaching the American level. Yet this growth has been achieved with few natural resources. The Japanese import 75 per cent of their energy, 99 per cent of their iron ore. They have few raw materials and need to import large quantities of food.

One of the effects of this unprecedented Japanese success in manufacturing has been the recognition by Western (and particularly American) management that there are more effective ways of managing than those taught in American business schools, and practiced in their factories. The reaction to this recognition has been to try to find out what the secret is. Dozens, possibly hundreds of senior executives have crossed the Pacific during the late 1970s and early 1980s to visit Japanese plants and to learn their secrets. The Japanese have been welcoming and frank. They have shown all they have to show, and talked openly about their management philosophy. Most of these executives have returned believers, some as evangelists. They have written reports. Because these reports are confidential (the Americans are not as open as the Japanese) few have been published, but they make fascinating reading. A great deal of this chapter is based on the discussions contained in these reports. The theme of the chapter is that the most important reason for the Japanese's success at managing large 'role' organisations is that they have achieved a high level of commitment from their organisation members.

The next section lists the ways in which they appear to have achieved standards of performance qualitatively higher than those to which the West has aspired. The following section describes the Japanese approach to the management of human resources. The section 'Japanese and teamwork' discusses the capacity of the Japanese to work together in teams and also considers if the Japanese success can be explained by unique cultural factors. The section 'Quality circles' discusses one of the ways with which the Japanese tap the capacities and wisdom of all their employees – through quality circles. The final section draws these themes together and presents a thesis that the Japanese are operating management principles that have been well known in the West for over two centuries. The Japanese have plagiarised Western ideas, and in typical Japanese fashion have made them work better than the originators.

The Japanese success has been in manufacturing industry and particularly in large organisations within the manufacturing sector. Japanese organisations in government, or the service sector do not have the same worldwide reputation for effectiveness. Westerners find the Japanese civil service notoriously bureaucratic and unimaginative. The Japanese seem to be able to manage 'role' organisations in a competitive environment in a way which allow them to continuously adjust to the threats and opportunities of the commercial world, and to continuously search for better ways of doing things, but they do not seem to have a style that suits the small entrepreneurial 'power' culture. Some care must be taken, therefore in applying the lessons the Japanese have to teach us. They could well not apply to all types of organisational cultures. On the other hand, they are undoubtedly relevant to the manufacturing organisations who find that they cannot compete with the Japanese, or who await with consternation, the entry of the Japanese into their section of the market.

The descriptions of the manufacturing systems and the management styles contained in this chapter are descriptions of what happens in the large Japanese organisations: the Mitsubishis and the Toyotas. They do not apply to many of the smaller manufacturing organisations, and certainly not to organisations outside the commercial manufacturing sector.

Japanese manufacturing system

Observers of the Japanese scene identify a number of key areas where the better Japanese organisations appear to have made quantum advances over their Western counterparts. Essentially these advances fit into three categories. The Japanese have been able to produce higher quality goods, with less capital employed, and at lower manufacturing cost.

Quality

The Japanese are producing goods that give fewer quality problems and last longer. These achievements stem directly from the Japanese emphasis on quality of the goods they produce and the way the achievement of quality is managed. In the plants the shopfloor operator accepts responsibility for his own quality. There are few inspectors, it is simply assumed that a component or assembly will not be passed on unless it is right. Any employee can stop a manufacturing process or an assembly track if there is a quality problem. Customer satisfaction comes first. The Japanese therefore achieve less waste (scrap) have fewer people to inspect the finished product, lower warranty costs and more repeat business from satisfied customers. All are major money savers.

Capital employed

The amount of work in progress and the number of semi-finished goods in stores is known technically as the company's inventory. The amount of inventory found in the Japanese plant is between 25 and 30 per cent of that normally found in equivalent American and European plants. The Japanese therefore need less working capital, less storage space, and fewer people controlling stores and moving materials. They have achieved these standards by refusing to have buffer stocks to be held in reserve in case problems occur. To the Japanese having no stocks means that quality must be right or the system breaks down – and that is the best way to ensure it never does break down. The 'right-first-time' philosophy is also carried over to relationships with suppliers. In an assembly area the supplier is expected to deliver components of the highest quality when and where the company needs them. The supplier will normally be based within a few miles of the plant. He may deliver directly to the track several times a day. His materials are not checked: quality is assumed. Frequently no delivery note will be signed; they will be felt to be unnecessary. The supplier is trusted to have it 'right-first-time' and deliver 'just-in-time'. The company has the benefit of low inventory and no requirements for stores, stores personnel or complex clerical recording systems.

Cost reductions

The Japanese achieve cost reduction targets that are far in excess of levels normally looked for in the West. They seem to be able to continuously reduce the level of materials being used, the costs involved in the manufacturing process, and the amount of waste being generated. They do this through a constant stress of searching for a better way of doing things, and through the involvement of all the organisations' personnel, at all levels, in looking for a better way. The extensive use of suggestion schemes (a large percentage of suggestions are used) and of quality circles are the principal mediums for identifying areas for cost reductions.

An analysis of these three main areas where the Japanese have proved so successful suggests that their secret lies in the way they manage their people. They are more effective because they do two things much better:

1 They problem solve. They manage in a way that brings problems to the surface so that these problems can be understood and plans for a solution developed and implemented. The Japanese emphasise a problem solving sequence: plan – do – check – action. The Westerner is all too willing to hide his mistakes, keep his problems to himself. That keeps the boss from his back, but it does not lead to improvements.

2 They utilise the talent for all their employees in a continuous search for better ways of doing things. They seem to have achieved a labour force that is more committed to the organisation, and more willing to put their talents and energies into bringing about organisation improvement than is their Western counterpart.

It can be argued that the major achievement that has emanated from the way the Japanese do things is not efficiency, but flexibility. All employees are orientated towards solving problems and finding a better way, so when problems occur due to changes in the environment – commercial, technical, social, political – all the efforts of the people are directed towards finding solutions to these problems rapidly and efficiently. How the Japanese achieve this, and how the lessons can be incorporated into the way we manage in the West, is the theme of this chapter and this book.

The Japanese also use the latest advances in technology to achieve their high standards of efficiency. Japanese factories are highly automated using the very latest (Western) technology. Computerised material and process control is an essential part of the efficient management of inventory. They use the highest standards of preventative maintenance. There are also economic factors which favour the Japanese. The Japanese banking system is more risk taking than its Western counterpart and is highly supportive of Japanese manufacturing. Most companies are financed through 80 per cent debt and 20 per cent equity. This allows them to be much less concerned with shareholders and more with the corporate community. The pressure for immediate results is low which gives the organisation the ability to sacrifice short-term profits for long-term gains.

The use of technology and the support of the banking system are important in understanding the causes of the Japanese success. They are not included in the list of key areas where the Japanese have made 'quantum' advances because the best of Western organisations can match the Japanese. They too use technology effectively and finance their organisations long term. But few, if any, Western organisations can match their Japanese competitors in quality, control of manufacturing costs and cost reductions. Few, if any Western organisations have achieved workforces as committed to problem solving and finding a better way. Few if any Western organisations have the Japanese capacity to react rapidly and flexibly to changes in the commercial environment: to manage change. These, then are the key things we should be looking at. To understand the Japanese success in these areas we must look at the way the Japanese manage their human resources, and how they achieve the capacity to work together in teams for the benefit of the organisation.

Japanese approach to managing people

Visitors to Japan report that the Japanese, when talking to their Western guests about the secret of their success, are very honest. They talk about their philosophy, and discuss the differences between Japanese and Western approaches. Visitors feel the biggest culture shock when discussion turns to the priorities of the Japanese manager during his day-to-day activities.

Priority 1 – The welfare of employees
Priority 2 – The image of the company in society
Priority 3 – The well-being of suppliers
Priority 4 – Profits

To the Westerner the profits represent both the reason for the enterprise's existence, and the way its success is measured. To the Japanese the profits will come if the first three priorities are met. If the company has a committed workforce, is well thought of within the society in which it operates and has a trusting relationship with its suppliers, then financial success will follow automatically. This section is about how the Japanese provide for the welfare of their employees, and about how they are able to maximise the useful contribution of their human resources towards the overall welfare of the organisation. Again it should be emphasised, this description only refers to the larger organisations within Japanese manufacturing industry and would not apply to many of the smaller companies or to organisations outside manufacturing.

The main characteristics of the Japanese approach to the management of their human resources are as follows:

Employment conditions

The Japanese employee has security. He is employed for life. Labour turnover is very low; employees rarely leave of their own accord and dismissal is virtually unheard of. Pay increases are by seniority – there are no differences in pay between different jobs and in some plants the same pay for skilled and semi-skilled work. Up to 33 per cent of total earnings is paid as a productivity bonus. A significant percentage of remuneration also comes in fringe benefits: subsidised housing, health, schooling, loans, sports and social activities. Retirement is early: 55–60. With their emphasis on seniority and stability, employment conditions in Japan, have more in common with the civil services, than with large manufacturing companies.

Recruitment and induction

Because employment is for life, a great deal of care is taken during the recruitment programme. If the image of the company is high in the community, the demand for employment within the company is high. The company is then able to recruit the best educated amd most intelligent young people. A great deal of time and effort is spent in the process of matching individual qualities to the needs of the company. Recruitment of new employees takes place once a year in order to facilitate the systematic induction (which lasts at least six months) and training of new employees.

Flexibility

The 'hired for life' commitment give the Japanese problems of flexibility in conditions of rapidly changing demand for labour. They manage this problem in a number of ways:

1 The employee is expected to be highly flexible, and to turn his hand to any task if his normal job is not needed.
2 The company employs a large number of contractors to do the more menial jobs, or to provide extra (temporary) labour in times of high demand. The contractor's employees do not have the same conditions of employment as the company employees, nor do they have the same security. Tasks for which there is a varying demand are contracted out.
3 Women and those who have retired are used as a pool of flexible labour to be called on as needed and discarded when the demand has been reduced.

The employees of a large Japanese manufacturing company represents an élite – carefully selected, systematically developed, well paid, protected and secure. Many, perhaps the majority, of Japanese do not have these working conditions.

The Japanese have also been able, even during recession periods, to maintain demand for their products more effectively than many companies in the West. The need for flexible working practices (and particularly for shedding excess labour) has, therefore been much less acute.

The emphasis on training and development in the Japanese organisation also leads to a highly flexible workforce. Job rotation is the norm at all levels. When a shopfloor worker has mastered a job, he will be transferred to another one to increase the number of his skills. Senior managers will have had experience of most, if not all, the functions in the organisation as their careers progressed. Junior managers find themselves being transferred from job to job. Some of these jobs they find tedious, but they build a well-rounded company man. The more skills and knowledge that are available within the organisation, the more flexible that organisation can be, because the people have the capacity to turn their hands and minds to many different tasks.

Management

Most managers are graduates, few are promoted from the shop floor. Demand to get into the most prestigious organisations is high, and the companies are able to select the most able, intelligent and compatible of each years' graduates for management training.

Management effort is directed into three areas:

1. The development of policies and plans. The Japanese approach to decision making is characterised by a search for social consensus no matter how long it takes to arrive at a decision. Imposed decisions are anathema. Senior managers, give authority to the decisions laboriously arrived at by their subordinates, and coordinate the decisions' implementation (consensus decision making is discussed in further details in the next section);
2. The technology of production: Japanese factories are highly automated;
3. The encouragement of feelings of belonging and the motivation to do better; the management are experts at facilitating groups, and at encouraging the contribution of problem solving of all employees.

As interesting as what they do do, is an analysis of what they do not do:

1. They do not get involved in day-to-day production problems, that is the work group's responsibility;
2. They do not issue orders or instructions.

Managers in Japan are highly visible, offices are normally located on the shopfloor. Managers spend a great deal of time with the workers, and know them more personally than a Western manager would feel was appropriate.

Supervision

Advancement from the shopfloor to the levels of supervision (normally four) is by seniority. But the supervisor as he achieves a higher level, does not gain any more authority to direct or instruct. His responsibility is to the development of his more junior colleagues: he takes an interest in their welfare, he helps with personal problems, he assists them to gain skills and knowledge, he ensures the right work ethics (teaching the company's ways). His role is more that of a father figure or benign counsellor than boss. The senior supervisors also have responsibility for the communication of production targets, of the company's progress, and of work standards. The supervisor works within the work group and is in some ways the assistant to the group, stepping in where problems occur, helping individuals who are having difficulties coping, and generally providing a flexible service to help where it is needed. His role is within rather than over the work group, but this does not imply that the role is not significant or the job does not carry a great deal of status and prestige.

Each worker is the responsibility of a more senior worker who is concerned with his health, welfare and commitment. But again probably of equal interest to the Western observer is what the supervisor is not responsible for: the responsibility for assignment of work, performance standards and discipline does not lie with the supervisor. That is the work group's responsibility.

Work group

Tasks are assigned to work groups, not individuals, and the group collectively accepts responsibility for the achievement of targets. The group sets objectives and monitors and records achievements. The responsibility to ensure quality (there are very few inspectors), cleanliness, minor maintenance, correct count, production on time, and elimination of waste lies with the group not the supervisor.

Any shopfloor problems invoke a problem solving discussion at which workers (including supervisors) with knowledge, experience and the desire to help, search for solutions. The work group also meets regularly to search for ways of doing things better (see section on 'Quality Circles').

The group collectively accepts responsibility for performance. The honour of the work group is of the highest importance; all its members are concerned with enhancing the group's image for high quality work. The members of the group socialise together, so the influence of work is much more pervasive to the Japanese worker than it is to his Western counterpart. In many ways it is the most important social contact in his life.

The group is also responsible for individual performance. If an individual group member is unable to cope with problems, his colleagues will work with him to ensure his skill increases. If a problem occurred over a group member's behaviour or attitude, the whole group's attention would be focused on bringing the erring one back into the fold. Formal disciplinary procedures are unheard of; the rejection of one of its members by the work group would lead to a serious problem of loss of face and also prestige.

Suggestion schemes

Central to their approach to the management of human resources, is the Japanese ability to maximise the contribution of their employees at all levels. This tapping of the wisdom of all their people is achieved through quality circles (discussed in section 'Quality circles') and through encouraging and utilising individual suggestions for improvements.

Japanese workers submit a large number of suggestions for improvements covering all areas of work (some plants quote an average of 8 per employee, per month). Management make a determined effort to use suggestions: rates varying from 50–90 per cent. Acceptance by management is seen as leading to employee satisfaction. Payment is sometimes made for the most effective suggestions – up to about £300.00. This reward is invariably used to benefit the group rather than the individual to whom the money was awarded. He may, for instance, take the group out for a social evening. The motivation for making suggestions is seen as primarily for the honour of the group, secondly for the honour of the family, and thirdly for improving company effectiveness.

Communications

The autonomous work group needs effective two-way communication. Communication upwards is largely through suggestion schemes and quality circles. Communication downwards ensures reinforcement of company values, philosophies and objectives, a clear understanding of targets and goals, and the building of a set of values shared by all employees. Senior supervisors are given the responsibility for ensuring effective communication, and the Japanese manager is clearly committed to open and effective communications.

Japanese and teamwork

Ruth Benedict, in her book *The Chrysanthemum and the Sword* discusses differences between the social attitudes of the Japanese and those of the Anglo-Saxon. Benedict was attempting to explain why Japanese soldiers, captured after often fanatical and suicidal resistance, during the Second World War could abruptly become willing helpers for their captors. Some Japanese are even reported to have flown to guide US bomb-aimers over their former units. Benedict suggested that a distinction exists between the Japanese and the Anglo-Saxons in terms of the individual's attitudes. In Japan, people tend towards collective action. They are highly motivated to seek the security of membership of a stable group, and the behaviour of individuals tends to be modified by their fear of group disapproval. Westerners prize independence, seek to exercise their individual initiative, and are regulated (more or less) by their own internal consciences. Not that the Japanese lack consciences, or that people in the West do not respond to group pressures. Rather, there is simply a difference of emphasis.

Benedict's conclusion, characterised as 'conscience *v* shame', has been debated widely in Japan. Certainly, it seems to illuminate how the group-directed attitudes of the average Japanese man cause so noticeable a difference between his pattern of life and that of, say, the average Briton. The British tend to separate their work from their other activities, and their friends, colleagues and family typically form distinct and different 'circles'.

For the Japanese, the natural and totally normal state of affairs is for a man's colleagues to be his friends, and the entirety of his friends – and vice versa. (Writing about 'men' is not sexist: in Japanese industry and management, far more even than in Britain, women are barred from the decision making levels of industry and commerce). Japanese men, whether they are office workers or managers (salary men) or factory workers spend a great deal of their 'free' time getting to know each other. They sit in bars and cabarets, go on outings, and eat endless snacks in the urban entertainment districts, as they talk about work, each other, work, work and work.

The outsider without much knowledge of the Japanese language might imagine that the bar, with its hostesses, music and free flowing whisky, is a place of entertainment. It is much more than this; the bar is an extension of the Japanese workplace, and one role of the hostess is to supply enough whisky to get the men talking. They learn about each other very thoroughly: they know each other's strengths (to be relied on) and weaknesses (to be managed). A group of men with this thorough mutual knowledge has a high potential for collective effectiveness. Even where the mutual knowledge is not high – for instance, between top management and factory floor workers – the 'collective' instincts of the people concerned minimise conflict and make group action highly effective.

This collective spirit of the Japanese allows them to be more effective than their Anglo-Saxon counterparts in three key areas: decision making, industrial relations, management of change.

Decision making

A set of proposal documents will be almost endlessly debated and analysed by all levels in the company hierarchy, until a consensus is reached. The company president will then give official approval to a decision already made by his juniors. The benefits of the Japanese system are that all the talents within the organisation will have been directed towards ensuring that the right decision has been made (or at least that key errors have been removed) and through participation all the people will feel commitment. All will have the knowledge to cooperate effectively to implement the new policy; all will be determined to make it work. The cost is the time taken to make decisions, the benefit is the ease and effectiveness of the decision's implementation.

Industrial relations

The annual wage negotiations in Japan are accompanied by a great deal of fire and brimstone. The rhetoric of the trade union leaders and the pessimism of the industrialists, as reported in the press and on television, would be entirely familiar to an American or European. Less familiar would be the half-day strikes, timed to cause least disruption and often followed by hours of unpaid work to recover any production lost during the strike. Also unfamiliar in the West would be the extraordinarily rapid achievement of consensus, and the fast settlement of disputes.

Japanese industrial relations practice is different in concept from the practices in the West where society is seen as divided between 'us' and 'them' (the typical description for the union – management dichotomy heard in the media is 'both sides of industry'). To the foreign eye, society in Japan certainly seems to be less class ridden and more cohesive than that. Most Japanese believe themselves to be 'middle-class' and refuse to admit that any important class division exists. Not only are the Japanese more cohesive, but their trade union structure encourages them to think of the welfare of the whole company.

Management of change

Western organisations during the last two decades have had major problems in introducing change, whether the change involves introducing new technology or revising personnel policies. The Japanese have managed change much more effectively. They have been poor at inventing new technology, but they are masters at taking other people's ideas and developing them and turning them into profit.

The reason for their success is not hard to find. Any major organisaation change (for instance the introduction of a new manufacturing process) will involve the integration of a number of complex processes and technologies. This integration is best managed by a group of people drawn from different disciplines working together as a team, rather than by a single man or woman. Since the Japanese are so good at teams, they are more consistently able to capitalise on new ideas (anybody's ideas). Where the native Western talent seems to be for invention and discovery (often by individual efforts) the Japanese are poor at these tasks. But once an invention or discovery is available, the Japanese can more often than not take it up, develop it and market it successfully and more quickly and with fewer errors and hitches than are experienced in the West.

The cohesive teamwork of the Japanese technological task force compares strikingly with Western native 'tribalism', where organisation members seem to behave as if they were fighting each other rather than the competition. The production tribe never trusts the marketing tribe; they both distrust the R & D tribe; and who (in his right mind) trusts the tribe of accountants?

This lack of ability to cooperate seems to stem from the Anglo-Saxon emphasis on individual worth which leads to feelings of insularity and low satisfaction from cooperative effort. Japanese team-work is more effective, because the team-members want to work together more than do their Western counterparts.

The capacity of the Japanese to work together in teams would seem to be one of the critical reasons why they are so successful at managing large organisations. Since business organisation is a system of interlocking human groups, the ability of people to work well in groups is obviously crucial. Management writers have been stressing the importance of effective group-working for many years; and in the environment of the 1980s, strong forces are at work which, if anything reinforce the need for group effectiveness. One such force is the increasing complexity of the modern technologies: exploiting the latest developments in process and product technology will almost always require the intelligent and enthusiastic cooperation of several people.

Western organisations would benefit, therefore, if they copy the Japanese approach to managing through teams. But is this Japanese approach transferrable? The Japanese, much more than the American or European it is argued, is naturally 'group' orientated rather than individualistic: he has a major concern with 'image' and 'face', with avoiding dishonour and his success is based on the group's success – nation, family, company, work group. Is the effectiveness of the Japanese factory based, as Ruth Benedict suggests, largely on this national capacity to work in teams to enhance prestige through effective performance? If so the Japanese would appear to have a built-in advantage, and the West will be unable to copy their approach.

The evidence that would question the 'national cultural advantage' thesis lies in two areas. Firstly, the Japanese organisation did not emerge naturally from cultural forces, but was based on Western ideas and concepts. Prior to the 1950s they adopted management styles that were highly authoritarian. The transition during the 1950s and 1960s was radical, but at the same time slow and systematic. It could well be that the Japanese culture took easily to the new ways of doing things, but the modern Japanese enterprise has been forged by thought, effort, patience and determination.

The second piece of evidence lies closer to home. The Japanese have been successful in their foreign investments and in grafting their management culture abroad, particularly into Britain. Visitors to most Japanese owned and managed factories in the UK find a disciplined, yet committed workforce. They find the typical Japanese emphasis on quality and problem solving. Communications are more open, union relations characterised by continuous dialogue. There will be no signs of status differences: all employees (including management) could well be wearing the same company uniform.

A number of Japanese labelled consumer goods are more likely to be assembled in Britain than their British labelled equivalents. They are also more likely to contain British made components. Investment in Britain by the Japanese has been steadily increasing. Any reservations on the part of the Japanese do not lie in their belief in their own ability to manage their factories, but in the capacity of their suppliers to meet commitments of quality and 'just-in-time' delivery. The concern is with the supplier's industrial relations, not their own.

The Japanese management style is therefore exportable, although British managers of Japanese owned companies will emphasise that a great deal of effort is made to adapt the Japanese style to the British environment. Western companies on the other hand have been singularly unsuccessful in importing Western management techniques into Japan. The only two major successes – IBM and McDonalds – both delegated the responsibility for the management of the enterprises to the Japanese.

Quality Circles

The ability of Japanese management to develop feelings of commitment amongst their people and the natural Japanese capacity for teamwork, has lead to the growth of effective problem solving and action planning activities by teams of organisation members at all levels. These activities have come to be known in the West as 'Quality Circles'.

A Quality Circle is a comparatively simple concept. It involves a group of people meeting together to identify and solve the problems they are having at work, and to identify improvements in the way things are done. In some ways the term 'Quality Circle' is a misnomer: the subject matter of Circles encompassed all areas of work – quality, delivery, costs, scrap etc. The membership of a Quality Circle is usually voluntary and restricted to work group members, although specialists may be called in to help with specific problems. Circle members are trained in analytical problem solving techniques, which develop a problem solving sequence as follows.

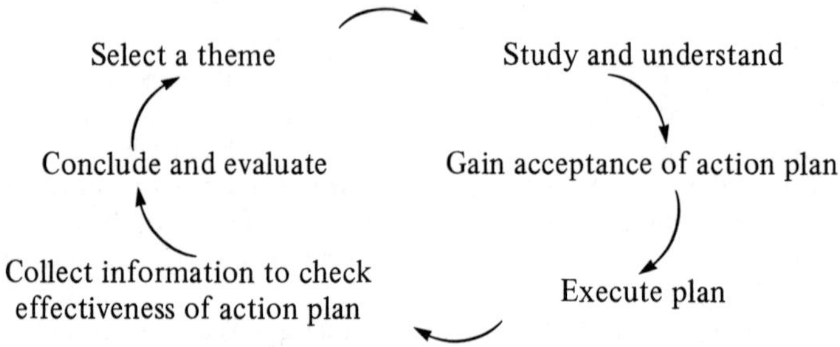

There are two broad categories of reasons for having Quality Circles in an organisation:

1 *Participation and involvement*: The quality circle offers an opportunity for all employees to become involved in making decisions about a central part of their life – their work. They will be influencing what happens to the jobs with which they are directly concerned, and they will be contributing towards the increased effectiveness of their own work area. The Quality Circle is a way of breaking down the 'don't care' attitudes and building involvement and commitment.
2 *Improved performance*: The Quality Circle assumes a problem solving approach. The Circle identifies its own problems (which perhaps someone else is trying to camouflage) and asks how things can be done better, i.e. improve quality, eliminate waste, provide the customer with a better product or service. It is perhaps this capacity to mobilise the whole workforce to strive for better ways of doing things that most differentiates the Japanese manufacturer, and is the most important single factor in accounting for the speed of Japanese advance.

Quality Circles were introduced in Japan in 1962. The original idea had come from America. The concept fitted in well with the style of management and the popularity of Circles grew rapidly. By 1980 it was estimated that there were over a million Quality Circles in Japan, involving ten million workers.

Again, a comparison between Japanese and British experience of Quality Circles is revealing. There are some 100-150 companies in Britain that claim to be using Quality Circles at present and the number is growing rapidly. The majority will fail and be abandoned; some will meet with partial success; a few will achieve their full potential. The reason for this disappointing outcome does not lie in the concept of the Quality Circle, but because their successful introduction requires that they become a way of life for everyone: part of the organisation culture. The successful introduction of Quality Circles requires a number of things to either be present or made to happen:

1 Senior management must believe that all their employees have a major contribution to make to improvements within their own work area. They must show this belief by finding time to listen to and consider proposals and by going out of their way to provide the resources to support implementation wherever this is practical. Top management understanding and commitment is the first priority.
2 Management must provide a facilitator to overview the development of the Circles. The facilitator must understand the nature of group dynamics. Many Circles fail because they contain people whose presence inhibits the development of work teams; specialists and managers. The facilitator must be a skilled and knowledgeable trainer: Quality Circles require a great deal of training support and the facilitator's job is to train Circle leaders. This is a time consuming process.
3 The 'leaders' of Quality Circles are usually supervisors. The supervisor must have the appropriate set of attitudes, and be given the appropriate skills. The leaders must have the capacity to train their people particularly in analytical problem solving and creative thinking, to encourage their contributions, and to build a team spirit.
4 Quality Circles must be understood by all members of the organisation, and must be supported by all the interest groups. Unions clearly have the capacity to inhibit their developments. Specialists are needed to advise and support the Circles, and often feel threatened by shopfloor people tackling problems usually considered their province. The way Quality Circles are introduced is crucial. Overall consensus must be reached.

The successful introduction of Quality Circles therefore requires commitment, understanding, consensus, supporting action, resources, training, and must involve, to a greater or lesser extent, all employees within an organisation. But the starting point, the foundation on which the concept must be built, is the belief by management that employees are able to find the solutions to their own problems. Management must believe that time spent in meetings will pay dividends through increased productivity, lower waste, high quality, increased motivation. They must genuinely delegate authority and responsibility; they must support but not interfere.

Prior to 1949 Japan was operating none of the systems that have subsequently proved so successful. They had copied the West and adopted Taylorism: a management élite and a subservient workforce. During the 1950s the Japanese deliberately rejected 'scientific management' in the light of an increasingly educated workforce. They read and believed the American literature which said that the old ways would lead to growing disinterest, low commitment, decrease in efficiency, increase in defects, higher labour turnover and absenteeism. Quality Circles came after years of development of participatory management style. The organisation had to be ready before they could take root and flourish. Once they succeeded they fed upon their own success. The people felt more and more involved and committed, the defects became fewer, the productivity became higher, the overheads became lower; job satisfaction and organisational efficiency advanced together. Quality Circles are not only a technique, they reflect a way of organisational life. The Quality Circles that fail to thrive in Britain will be in organisations whose cultures are not capable of nourishing them, and whose managers take a traditional view of the worker as a troublesome, but necessary extension to an efficient machine.

Quality Circles require that the organisation culture emphasises the involvement of employees at all levels in the decisions that affect them and that the management believe in the potential contribution of all employees to increasing effectiveness.

Summary and conclusions

The Japanese organisations, then, are different in many ways from their Western counterparts. Japanese manufacturing organisations have been conspicuously successful over the last fifteen years, and this success has had serious implications for the prosperity of their Western competitors. It is important we understand the reasons for this success, and identify which of the Japanese ways we can, and should, adopt in the West. It is up to the senior management of each organisation to understand how the Japanese work and to choose and adapt those aspects which can be used to improve the long-term effectiveness of their organisation.

The aspects of the Japanese way of working which are selected should lead to increased effectiveness in three areas: commitment, efficient use of resources, and flexibility. From the material presented in this chapter, the main ways in which the Japanese achieve these three critical objectives can be summarised as follows.

Commitment

1 The Japanese worker is hired for life and has few opportunities to change employers. He has little choice but to become committed to his company. The American manager changes employers some eight times more often than his Japanese counterpart.
2 The emphasis on welfare and personal growth develops trust and mutual indebtedness.
3 The employee's major social relationships are with his work colleagues and great efforts are made to acquaint all employees with company values.
4 The larger Japanese organisations are highly prestigious: employees are proud to be members.
5 The Japanese worker feels that he is making a contribution: management put time and resources into using all their employee's talents.

Efficiency

1 There is a constant emphasis on getting work groups to think about how to do things better: the wisdom of all employees is utilised.
2 The commitment to giving quality highest priority leads to increases in efficiency in all other areas.
3 The Japanese organisation is able to integrate the efforts of all employees through the mechanisms of close human relationships. The Western approach, through hierarchy and standard procedures, seems less effective.
4 The Japanese work closely with suppliers and are able to integrate the action of different organisations.
5 Training and development programmes ensure high levels of technical skills.
6 The larger Japanese organisations can afford to be highly selective in their choice of employees.

Flexibility

1 The Japanese have developed a number of techniques for accommodating to changing demand for labour: temporary and part time employment of women, use of contractors for

'one-off' jobs or work with variable demand, employment of retired persons for temporary upturns in demand.

2 The resources allocated to training and the emphasis on job rotation has led to a workforce with many and versatile skills.

3 The high levels of commitment to Company success has inhibited the development of inflexible work practices.

4 The large percentage of income paid as a bonus means that the labour costs drop radically during a business downturn.

Ouchi summarises the main differences between the organisation that uses a Japanese style of management (Theory Z) and the organisation that uses a Western style of management (Theory A) as follows:

Topic	*Theory A*	*Theory Z*
Size of work units	Large to maximise economy of scale	Small to maximise communications and flexibility
Quality	Comes from systematic checks and tests	Comes from individual commitment
Consensus management	Consensus produces camels where horses are needed	Quality, efficiency and creativity comes through teamwork
Specialisation	Brings productivity	Brings inflexibility
Achievement	High pay and rapid promotion motivates high flyers	Motivation comes from commitment through involvement in decision making
Control	Maintained by external discipline	Maintained through conformity to shared values
Career growth	Between different organisations in the same specialisation	Between specialisations in a single organisation

To Ouchi the 'vision' that the senior management of Western organisations should adopt is Theory Z.

The evidence is growing that the Americans and Europeans are becoming more and more aware that there are many aspects of the Japanese collectivism that can be successfully copied, and that, if new policies are followed consistently and with determination, relevant Japanese techniques can be brought across the Pacific. These new policies include:

1 Recruiting and promoting people on the basis of their ability and willingness to work within teams.

2 Delegating decision making and policy development to project teams.
3 Inviting lower levels of management to become collectively involved in strategic planning by using a workshop approach. This involves deliberately giving up the advantages of top management decision making (it is rapid, easily controlled and makes the top managers feel good) for the advantages of group decision making (it leads to understanding, trust, cooperation and commitment). It also involves living with the disadvantages of group decision making (it is slow and takes up a great deal of management time; time that therefore cannot be made available to address day-to-day short-term problems).
4 Rewarding planning and teamwork rather than 'not giving me a problem today'. This requires senior management spending a great deal of their time reviewing the plans developed by the management teams. It requires that senior management avoid becoming involved in the day-to-day problems.
5 Improving team effectiveness. This can have a far reaching effect on both the overall team performance and the understanding by individual team members of the value of group decision making. Team building techniques can play a big role in improving the performance of our organisations.
6 Taking a more consultative approach with trade unions, and helping them to think about the long-term welfare of the organisation. Chapter Ten reviews how this might be achieved.
7 Involving employees at all levels in making a contribution to increasing the effectiveness of their work environment, so that all the human potential of the organisation can be tapped. Many Western companies are embracing the Japanese concept of the quality circle, and the rapidity with which the use of quality circles is growing illustrates the willingness of Western industry to incorporate foreign ideas that work.

There is nothing new in any of these ideas. No new approach to management is required: rather the conscientious application of the methods preached by many management gurus (Blake, Drucker, Herzberg, McGregor) over many years. The 'Quality of Working Life' movement, autonomous work groups, job rotation, socio-technical approaches, job enrichment are all intimately related to the Japanese approach to the management of human resources. The Japanese apply the simple ABC's of management well, consistently, at all levels, and long term. The management philosophy was being practiced by Robert Owen in his Lanarkshire mills in the 1780s. The West have forgotten these ideas, the Japanese resurrected them. In some industries more than others, the Westerners have a long way to go to catch up. The Japanese are teaching us that until we can all cooperate as a team, we will not take naturally to the business environment of the 1980s. This book is about how to go about developing an organisation which takes on some of the characteristics which the Japanese have demonstrated to give a competitive advantage.

PART TWO
THE ORGANISATION DEVELOPMENT PROCESS

Overview

So far we have argued that if our organisations are going to increase their competitiveness, we need to develop new ways of managing our human resources. We have also stated what characteristics we should be aiming for in these new organisations:

1. An action planning and problem solving approach;
2. High levels of commitment by all the organisation's members;

so that the organisation is able to adjust rapidly to changes in its environment, solve the problems it is having and take advantage of any opportunities for increased efficiency.

We now turn to how we achieve the new organisation. Part One of this book discussed what we should be aiming for, Part Two explains how to get there.

Once we have a clear idea of the organisation culture we want to develop, what strategies do we have to employ to transform our organisation from what it is now to what we want it to be in the future?

In Part Two, action in a number of areas will be discussed. All this action is designed to bring about this transformation from traditional to committed cultures. It will be argued that the change process requires that:

1. We have new organisation structures;
2. We involve all the people in the change process in order to increase their knowledge and skills, and develop feelings of commitment;

3 We develop new systems, particularly in communications, participation and remuneration;
4 We move towards managing through teams;
5 We manage work so that people are able to make a more significant contribution, particularly through the introduction of job redesign, group working and quality circles;
6 We put a great deal of effort into training and developing all the organisation members.

Action in all these areas, at the right time and in the right way will, over time, lead to a new culture. These strategies for effecting change will be illustrated by a case study. We will follow the process of organisation development in an imaginary organisation, which we can call company X. Throughout this case study we shall illustrate how the change process can be managed, what it feels like to be involved in a change process, what the problems are and how they can be overcome, the conflicts, hostility and heartaches a major change programme can cause, and the principles that must be followed.

Our case study is set in a manufacturing plant. Company X is one of four plants that together make up the corporation. Corporation X operates in the heavy end of the automotive market, and all the plants both manufacture and assemble. The corporation has a reputation for producing quality (but expensive) products and for technological innovation.

Company X employs some 3,000 people in a medium-size English town, where they are seen as good and fair employers. The plant is some 20 years old and has been producing much the same range of products during this period. Profits have been steady but not spectacular.

The corporate management had spent a great deal of time, over many years, developing their own views on how their plants should be managed in the future. The driving force behind this thinking was the managing director. He had taken a great deal of interest in the way the Japanese manage, and had read widely in the fields of management and organisation theory. He had been impressed by the emphasis that Theory Z puts onto developing clear corporate values. At a series of seminars, the corporate management had developed and recorded their vision of how they saw the culture they wished to see developed in their plants. This vision became known as the 'corporate management philosophy'. It contained many of the ideas found in Part One of this book.

One of the plants – at Flagtown – has been operating for only two years. The corporate management had made great efforts to build their 'corporate management philosophy' into the organisation design and the management style of Flagtown. They believe that this experiment has been successful. They now feel that they must attempt to pursue the achievement of the same organisation culture at their older, more traditional plants like company X.

The corporation see company X as efficient, but conservative and with most of the characteristics of Handy's 'role' culture. Corporate management have concerns that company X will not be sufficiently flexible to meet the changing and more competitive environment they envisage in the next decade. The plant manager, who is a member of the corporate management team, has discussed this with his boss, the managing director. They have agreed a plan that is designed to ensure in company X, long-term organisation development.

Part Two describes how this plan works out in practice to produce a more committed, flexible and effective organisation.

Company X does not exist. The restructuring, the workshops, the systems development, the training programme described in Part Two never took place, although they could have done. The material used to construct our change process in company X has been taken from experiences of many change processes in many organisations in order to illustrate the sorts of changes that can be achieved in practice if the process of change is managed effectively.

A case study approach to describe the process of organisation change has been chosen because it puts the flesh on the analytical skeleton of theory and principle. It will make the change process more meaningful and live for the practical, results orientated manager who spends his time in commercial organisations and who understands, at least intuitively, how they work. Hopefully because of the case study approach, this practical manager will be more able to gauge the value for his organisation of this process of managing change.

The case history may not be so meaningful for readers who do not have direct experience in the private sector. The need for the committed, flexible organisation is however no less in central government, local government, hospitals, schools, nationalised industries, or the armed forces, and the principles and techniques still apply. It is hoped that all readers, whether or not they have direct experience of private sector organisations, will find that the case history helps to provide practical insight into what needs to be done.

4 Organisation Design and the Committed Culture

This chapter discusses ways of structuring organisations to facilitate the development of a committed culture. Only some aspects of organisation design and organisation structure will be discussed: those that are directly related to the achievement of the committed culture, and without which that culture will be difficult if not impossible to achieve. There are three objectives which the organisation designs suggested in this chapter are intended to achieve:

1 The facilitation of a delegatory management style;
2 The growth of teamwork;
3 The integration of functions.

Each of the proposals makes a contribution to all three of these objectives.

In company X the corporate management decided that the first step in the organisation development programme was a reorganisation. They considered that this reorganisation should take place before any attempt was made to involve the management of the plant in the programme. There was a belief at corporate level that the problems of organisation structure must be tackled first. The restructuring was aimed to reduce hierarchy, reduce the emphasis on functional autonomy, and produce smaller units. This chapter summarises the arguments on which the corporate management based their plans for restructuring.

Hierarchy

Organisations vary in the number of levels between the shopfloor (or 'doers') and the top management. Before the organisation development programme there were seven levels in company X. The plant manager knew that available research* suggested that this was about average for Western organisations with about 3,000 members. The corporate strategy was to move to five levels: shopfloor operator, supervisor, middle manager, senior manager and plant manager. The belief behind this strategy was that reducing the number of levels would bring about a number of advantages and would help to produce a culture based on delegation and trust. It was also believed that the problems generated by flat structures (i.e. low hierarchy) could be managed.

The advantages of having fewer levels in an organisation hierarchy are as follows:

1 Fewer levels lead to more delegation:
  (*a*) Low hierarchies and flat structures mean high span of control and therefore each manager and supervisor will have more people reporting to him;
  (*b*) The more people that report to a manager or supervisor, the more responsibility he will have;
  (*c*) The more responsibility he has, the more he is obliged to delegate, because there is a limit to the amount he can personally achieve;
  (*d*) People (both bosses and subordinates) respond positively to the challenge of exercising more responsibility and to having more scope to their job. More delegation leads to increased discretion and more scope for individual achievement.

  On the other hand, taller structures lead to closer supervision, greater control over subordinate discretion, and the greater likelihood that work will be gone over again by the boss. Flatter structures reduce the ability of the boss to operate direct control, oblige him to increase his trust in his subordinates to operate effectively. The committed organisation requires high levels of mutual trust.

2 Fewer levels mean easier and more efficient communications. Very often when managers complain that they have problems communicating with operators and supervisors, one finds that they are operating with a tall structure. Communications become distorted in passing up and down many levels.

---

* See Child J. *Organisation*, Harper and Row, 1977, pp. 50–54

Instructions become diluted or reinterpreted. In passing up information, there is a well-known tendency to present communications in terms that will least offend the recipient.

3 Organisations with low hierarchy have fewer managers and are therefore cheaper. In effect the productivity required of each manager is increased through increasing his span of control.

4 Low hierarchy leads to greater administrative clarity. In structures with many levels of management, it is more difficult to distinguish discrete levels of responsibility and authority between positions at adjacent points in the hierarchy. High levels of performance require that authority is clearly defined, and that each individual knows his areas of responsibility and accountability. Not knowing where you stand can be very demotivating, and is more likely to occur in tall structures.

If the aim is to produce a committed and flexible organisation culture, flat structures are therefore a prerequisite. There are, however, disadvantages in reducing the number of levels in an organisation. The main factors limiting the flatness of structures are:

1 *The competence of subordinates*: The greater the competence of subordinates, the greater the potential span of control. Limited competence means that the boss must spend a great deal of his time in coaching, counselling and in other ways developing the capacities of those who work for him. He therefore must restrict the number of his subordinates to a number he can train and develop effectively. As the competence of subordinates rise through experience and training, it becomes feasible to widen spans of control and reduce levels of management.

2 *The complexity of the task*: In a high technology environment, managers will be supervising people with extensive and disparate knowledge and roles. These environments tend to be rapidly changing. There will be new problems to tackle, a range of specialist skills to draw upon and to coordinate, and probably a large call on the supervisor's or manager's time to advise on difficult technical and operational matters. This complexity will reduce the capacity of the manager to take on a large number of tasks. The converse is also true. A mass production system gives the ability to operate a larger supervisory span of control than does, for instance, a unit developing a prototype or constructing a one-off special order.

3 *The competence of the manager*: Managers who are good motivators, have subordinates who learn faster, who take on more responsibility, are more trustworthy, work more conscien-

tiously and need less supervision. The reverse is also true. Managers who are poor motivators have subordinates who need to be supervised more closely. The poor motivator will have a greater supervisory burden than the good motivator even though they have the same number of people. The width of the span of control, therefore, is limited by the capacity of the manager.

4 *The optimum size of effective teams*: The final reason for restricting spans of control is particularly relevant to building a committed organisation. We have emphasised the importance of teamwork and team building.

Work teams have optimum sizes, and once they grow above this size cohesion is reduced. This optimum size depends upon the complexity of the task. Where a great deal of innovation or development is undertaken, with large amounts of information and many uncertainties, a high degree of cohesion within the group of subordinates will be necessary. They will have to work closely and constructively together in a problem solving mode. Such a work team can provide the integration between different tasks that, in classical management theory, is part of the manager's job. But in such groups as size increases beyond about 7–8 members there is a tendency for faction or cliques to form generating conflict, and the participation of individual members falls off. There is a sound argument for restructing the number of subordinates per manager, therefore, to the number that can make a coordinated and cohesive team.

This section has concerned itself with only those aspects of organisations' hierarchy which relate closely to the achievement of a committed organisation. There are many other facets of this topic which are important to consider when deciding on the appropriate number of levels in an organisation. There are a number of good books on this subject; readers are referred to the reading list at the end of this book.

Integrating the functions

The corporate management's second objective in restructuring company X was to achieve a much better integration between the different functions or departments. Their thinking was influenced by some of Handy's ideas. Handy describes his 'role' organisation as resting on the strength of its pillars – its functions or specialities. The pillars are strong in their own right; the finance department, the purchasing department, the production facility, all may be internationally renowned for their efficiency. These pillars pursue their own objectives and this can lead to problems in coordinating their different tasks so that the organisation can be managed effectively. It can also lead to protection of the department's interests, rather than considering the interests of the organisation as a whole. Most people with experience in large organisations will have experienced the departmental managers who behave like robber barons, sapping the energy of the organisation with their internal conflicts. Scoring points off each other becomes more important than providing a service to the customer. To Handy this is one of the main reasons for the 'role' organisation's flexibility; 'They are slow to see the need to change and slow to change even when the need is seen'. Handy illustrates what he calls this 'functional myopia' with the following example.

> 'As director of a general management programme I was once in search of a so-called multi-disciplinary problem which would help the participants to understand the interlinking nature of the functional areas of management. It seemed to me that the recent much-publicized failure of a nationally-known firm would provide a good example. I suggest this to my colleagues on the teaching staff of the programme.
>
> 'Excellent idea,' said the economist, 'a classic example of the failure to forecast a peaking of the demand curb'.'
>
> 'Of course,' said the accountant, 'this organisation has never understood the concept of cash-flow – an excellent case-study'.
>
> 'I should be delighted to be involved,' said the organisation theorist, 'it only goes to show how inflexible a centralised organisation can become'.
>
> 'It's a bit too obvious, that's the only trouble,' said the marketing man, 'with their distribution system and pricing policy disaster was inevitable'.
>
> If all were right, I wondered could any one of them be more right than the others?'

In a manufacturing organisation the major conflicts are usually with the manufacturing or production function. They are blamed for not meeting targets and giving marketing a problem with their customer. They in turn blame purchasing for the supplier's poor quality or raw materials, or engineering for upsetting their routines by introducing new processes.

Manufacturing is also usually much larger than the other departments. In many engineering companies like company X the shopfloor operators are organised into a manufacturing department which could contain well over half the total organisation members. This size brings extra problems of hierarchy and communication.

The solution to the problem of integrating the functions which was introduced into company X also handles the problem of the large size of manufacturing departments. Because it is still a rare organisation phenomenon, it does not have a name in common use. In this description it will be called the 'business' approach because it sets out to form the organisation into a series of mini-businesses. The stimulus to developing a 'business' is to overcome these two problems commonly found in 'role' organisations – the conflict between departments and the problem of the number of people working in the manufacturing function. They achieve this by abolishing departments and breaking up the manufacturing function.

In a 'business' structure the manufacturing function is divided into a series of autonomous units, each assigned to a senior manager. The senior manager also has responsibility for one function or specialist service area, but this responsibility is for policy development, auditing, training and technical support; it is not for 'doing'. The 'doers' are allocated to the different businesses, where they are organised into manufacturing support teams. (This concept is discussed further in Chapter Ten which suggests that matrix management structures are needed to complement 'business' organisations and team working.)

Figure 4.1 presents the organisation chart view of the 'business' and compares old with new.

Business structures must be developed to meet the specific needs of each organisation, so will vary from one organisation to another. The business structure shown in Figure 4.1 would fit well into company X, where the manufacturing function is logically divided into five units, where it was felt that the marketing manager was away from the plant too often to be made responsible for a manufacturing area, and where plans for major engineering projects were being developed that would require the engineering manager to work full time in this work. This business structure freed one of the senior managers for a new innovating role.

The advantages for reorganising towards business structures are these:

1 The 'robber baron' syndrome disappears. Each department manager is now a business manager with responsibilities for an autonomous area of manufacturing plus providing a service to all the other business managers. Each business manager needs the services of his colleagues and must reciprocate by providing a service to them.
2 Communications are much improved because of the smaller units which allows the senior manager to be organisationally closer to the operators: he has fewer people, and fewer levels

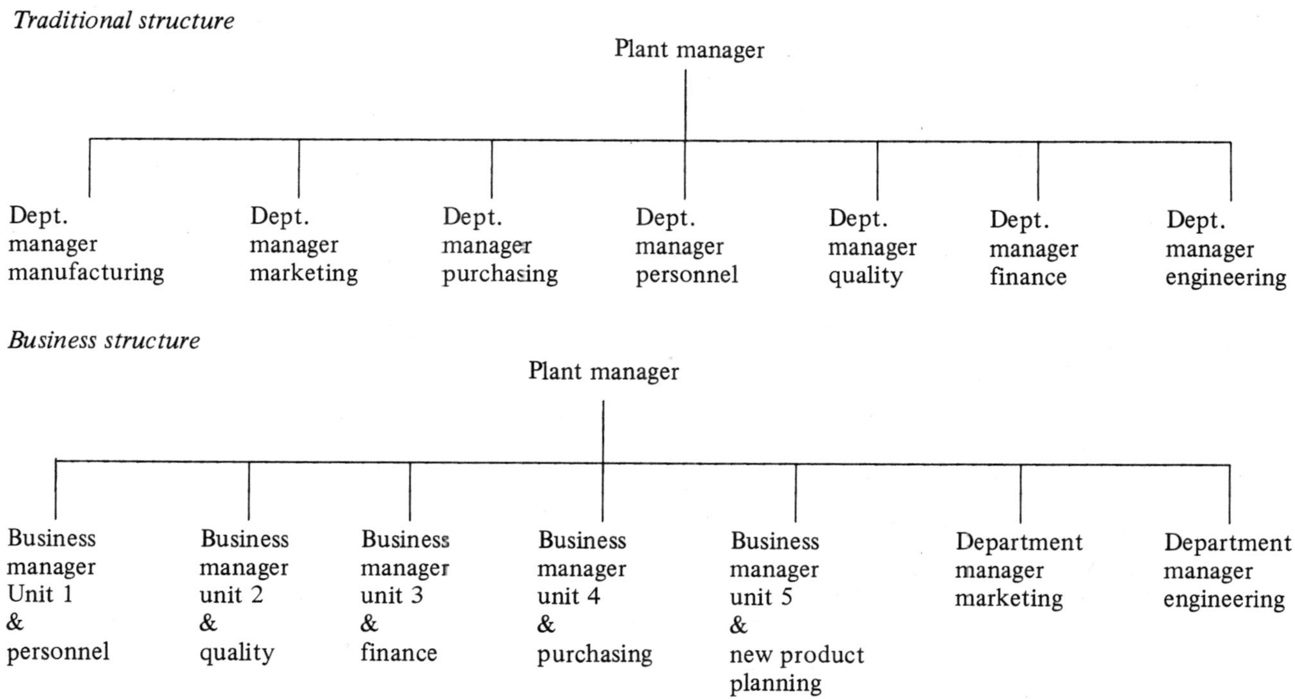

Figure 4.1 Comparison between traditional and 'business' structures

between himself and his operators.

3 The senior manager becomes 'despecialised'. He must take on new and different roles, and must accept new challenges and new learning. Movement to a business structure is broadening and therefore develops management skills. Moving to business structures is an extremely effective way of developing managers. The total 'pool' of managerial talents is increased and this gives extra flexibility to the organisation.

4 The 'business structure' is much more flexible than the classical structure. For instance the responsibility for Unit 3 can be transferred without any major upheaval to the engineering manager if the organisation emphasis on engineering innovation is reduced, and the plant manager wants the finance manager to work on an economic forecasting model. The finance manager will have gained his general management experience, and become a more effective manager because of it, and can be assigned to another manufacturing unit in the future. In a 'business' structure change and flexibility become the norm, and the senior management become less and less concerned with building or protecting an empire based on functional specialisation.

The introduction of business structures can be a traumatic affair; they represent a radical change in responsibilities for the senior management. They will not, however, be to the liking of all the senior managers. Managers who have limited man-management skills tend to retreat into functional specialisations and the business structures do not allow this to happen. They can expose people's weaknesses. But such exposures are one of the things that organisation development is about; the identification of problems so that action can be taken to solve them. In this case the problem is the limited abilities of a senior manager.

Summary and conclusions

The main points made in this chapter can be summarised as follows:

1 The way organisation member's jobs are organised can have an important impact on the development of a committed organisation culture. This chapter reviews the more important and relevant organisation design features necessary to support an organisation development programme.

2 Flat structures with low hierarchies encourages delegatory management styles, high trust levels, better communications and clearer definitions of responsibilities.

3 Organisations based on large functional departments tend to have poor integration of tasks and poor communication. 'Business' structures based on autonomous manufacturing units lead to better cooperation between functions, better communications, more individual development and more flexibility.

This chapter has discussed the changes in organisation design and organisation structure that should take place before embarking on a workshop approach to organisation development. The changes proposed have been described as being imposed by corporate management, without consultation with the people involved. Yet in Part One of this book we argued that the committed culture will only be developed in organisations which practice, over many years, a management style which emphasises the involvement of all organisation members in decision making in those areas of their working environment which is of direct concern to them. This anomaly will be explained in Chapter Five, which discusses the 'workshop approach'. In this chapter, it will be argued that although commitment will only come through involvement, consultation and participation, there are times when more authoritarian approaches are both necessary and appropriate in order to achieve change.

This chapter has described only the initial restructuring necessary to provide a foundation for the organisation development programme. As this programme progresses, further restructuring will take place, and new organisation designs will be introduced. These changes are described in Chapter Ten, which is concerned with team structures and team development. The adoption of 'business' structures suited company X. Such structures may well not be appropriate for other organisations, and would not be suitable for organisations working in a very different environment (e.g. service industries, organisations involved with higher technological innovation, public service). Nevertheless some form of restructuring is almost invariably needed as a foundation for an organisation development programme. The aim of this restructuring will be to reduce hierarchy, increase integration between functions and produce smaller working units.

5 The Workshop Approach to Organisation Development

Managing change in a typical 'role' organisation is a mighty task. Their nature is to be a steady state, to continue to do the things that they know they do well, even when those activities are no longer what is needed. The late 1970s and early 1980s have seen an increase in the pace of change in the environment within which these organisations work. Economic recession, a changing competitive environment, technological innovation, government economic policies are all factors in the organisation's environment to which they have had to adjust. Many organisations have failed to make the adjustment. Others have done so only at very great cost; financial and social. Some have managed the process of adjustment successfully and are strengthening their position in the market place. The Japanese seem to have been particularly successful in weathering the social and economic storms. They have been able to adjust to the changes in their environment much better than many of their American and European competitors.

This chapter is about an approach to the management of change: the 'workshop approach'. The approach is based on a number of principles or theories' about behaviour in organisations. It is also based on the observations of the way in which the Japanese (and some Western organisations) use these principles and put the theories into practice. The assumptions behind the workshop approach are:

1 An effective organisation will be developed if a policy of increasing the understanding and commitment of all the organisation's members is followed.

2 As understanding and commitment is established, organisation members will work towards increasing efficiency and flexibility.
3 Understanding and commitment can only come through effective communication and the involvement of employees at all levels in making decisions about, and influencing, the things of direct concern to them in their place of work.
4 Involving people implies an opportunity to work through issues and problems in a group situation, because people at work take their attitudes and beliefs from their peers – the people whom they feel are like them. In this book these group situations are called 'workshops'.
5 The commitment of management to the delegation of authority and responsibility, to effective communications, and to supporting group activities is essential. The leadership must come from the top.
6 For successful organisation development, the organisation must make structural and systems changes to complement workshop activities and must invest in training and development to provide new knowledge and skills.

There are many examples of organisation change, some successful, that have been achieved using very different principles. No claim is made that the workshop is the only approach, or even always the most appropriate approach. In times of crisis it would not be.

The workshop approach will develop, if operated consistently over a period of years, an organisation that automatically adjusts to its environment because all the organisations' members are sensitive to what needs to be done. This sensitivity is produced by having everyone committed to identifying and solving the problems that confront them and their colleagues during their work, and by having everyone searching for a better way of doing things. In such an organisation change is 'built in' to the day-to-day operations. The workshop approach then is not only a way of managing change, it is a way of developing an organisation whose chief characteristic is member commitment.

In the following section a workshop designed to begin the process of planned organisation development in company X is described. This workshop takes place after the restructuring described in Chapter Four has been implemented. The section on workshop principles describes the rules or principles that must be followed in order to achieve a successful outcome for a workshop. Each workshop is unique: differing from any other workshop in problems to be tackled, objectives to be met, background of participants and many other variables. But because workshops represent an approach to managing change, they are all guided by a set of principles which gives them a common approach.

Chapters Six, Seven, Eight, and Nine describe different sorts of workshops. Each is based on a model of change through consultation, participation, involvement and communications and each is designed to meet the principles set out in this chapter. Each of the workshops conform to the same principles, but each is tailor-made to take account of the unique nature of the problems to be tackled.

Workshop activities are intended to develop participation and consultation, and thereby increase the involvement of all the members of an organisation in the management of their work environment. This does not imply that workshops are designed to produce leaderless situations. The leader role is key, but he does not make operating decisions, he facilitates decision making by others. He decides what management style will be used, he stimulates the development of the commitment of his people, he guides the organisation development programme in that part of the organisation for which he is responsible, he has the vision of the future. Because workshop activity goes on in all areas and at all levels of the organisation that leader might be a plant manager, a school headmaster, a hospital administrator, a department manager, a union leader or a supervisor. In fact, he will be anyone with responsibility for maximising the performance of part of an organisation.

The person who takes the responsibility for a development programme to any degree within an organisation is given the title of 'headman' in this book. The headman is the leader of a workshop. The role of the headman is discussed in more detail later in this chapter.

The planning workshop

The atmosphere in company X had been difficult for some months. Even senior management did not know what was happening or why. They knew that a reorganisation was coming but they had not been consulted. They knew that some would benefit, some would lose out, but had no idea who. When the new structures, and the new top management positions and their encumberants were announced the tension was relieved; at least now they knew where they stood. But no-one understood the reasons for the new organisation design. Only the plant manager and corporate management had been involved. Once the new structures were announced it was time, the plant manager decided, to involve the total management group in managing the change process. He believed that the best way to initiate this was through a workshop. He planned this workshop with the help of a consultant who was made responsible for making the necessary administrative arrangements and for managing the workshop programme. The plant manager took the role of headman.

Rooms in a local hotel were hired for two days. All the management team were invited. This was the first culture shock. In the old days it would have been seen as irresponsible for two managers within the same department to be out of plant on the same day. Now the plant was expected to run without a single executive or manager (needless to say, it ran like clockwork). The plant manager believed that by leaving the plant to be run by supervisors he was actively demonstrating his determination that in future the role of the manager would be to think and plan, not to deal with the day-to-day. He was also determined that all the management group would be responsible collectively for managing the change process.

The day arrived, and the management team collected at the hotel. The atmosphere was one of both apprehension and anticipation. In the room a table was set out to form a long horseshoe. At the head of the horseshoe was a flip chart, video player and a table for the presenter. The day began with a brief welcome from the plant manager acting as headman, and then an explanation of the objectives of the day and a description of the programme by the consultant. (The objectives of the workshops are given in Figure 5.1). Silence! A video tape recorded by the managing director was then played. The video explained the corporate management philosophy and how and why he believed company X needed to change in order to meet the demands of the future. The atmosphere was quiet but attentive. A written summary of the main points made in the presentation was given to each delegate.

1 To inform management about:

– the reasons for the recent restructuring;
– the corporate management philosophy.

2 To consult with the management group on the advantages and disadvantages of the corporate management philosophy.

3 To begin the process of involvement of the management group in developing policies and procedures to implement the organisation development programme, in particularly by:

– identifying problems to be overcome;
– developing action plans to tackle these problems.

Figure 5.1 Planning workshop objectives

The workshop was then asked to divide into departmental teams. Each department was asked to go away to a separate room and discuss their reaction to the tape; and what they felt about the corporate philosophy. Armed with coffee and biscuits and a flip chart the management group split up into their teams and left the meeting room for their syndicate discussions. Fifteen minutes later the consultant went round to ensure that they all understood the task (they did) but otherwise they were left alone. At the end of one-and-a-half hours they reassembled. Each group had nominated one of their members to present a summary of their discussions.

The presentations were hard hitting. A great deal of management frustration was revealed; it was made clear that the management group felt that it had been unfairly treated. There was some distrust and suspicion shown, and implicit in some of the comments were criticisms of how the plant manager had handled the organisation restructuring. The tape had included statements about principles of restructuring and why restructuring was believed necessary to develop more flexible and reactive organisations. This material was new to most of the managers. The tape also contained statements about managing the organisation's human resources so that greater use is made of the potential contributions of employees at all levels in the organisation. The spokesmen pointed out the contradiction between a commitment on the part of top management to employee participation and the way the management group had had the reorganisation imposed upon them. On the other hand the corporate philosophy statement was well received and seen as an opportunity. The managers believed that corporate management were doing their job and providing a strategic framework in which to operate. It was also clear that the management did not fully understand the corporate philosophy, and were unclear on how it could be turned into practical day-to-day management techniques.

The headman kept a 'low profile' during this part of the workshop. He sat in the chair vacated by the spokesmen rather than at the head of the horseshoe. He did not try to counter the criticisms. He did not give explanations unless he was asked direct questions. When he spoke it was to ask for clarification of points made or to ask for an expansion of the ideas being presented. As time went on the presentations became less to the plant manager, more to the group as a whole. The presentations became less formal, the presenters less self-conscious, and the managers were more willing to contribute towards group discussions.

Lunch was a buffet which allowed the delegates to continue their informal discussions and to circulate. Discussions tended to be a continuation of the topics that had been presented in the final session and people circulated to test the opinions of their peers in a less public atmosphere. The headman was having his ear bent by two or three of the younger managers, but their older companions were more circumspect and did not risk too wholesome criticism. He was after all the 'boss'. The headman continued his role of listener – he asked for clarification and expansion of the points that were being put to him, he did not argue or try to put down his junior colleagues.

The afternoon session began with a presentation from the headman. The consultant had listened to the departmental presentations in the morning and recorded where he believed there was a lack of understanding of the corporate philosophy, or where it seemed more information was needed. He had gained the delegates' agreement that the list represented their information needs at the end of the morning session and had the list typed and duplicated during lunch. The plant manager took the list and attempted to provide explanations and illustrations. He was only partly successful. It became clear from the questions and comments that the concern of the management group was that the corporate philosophy was 'theory': all very well for the top brass to pontificate, but would it work in practice? They wanted concrete examples of where the principles had been used in real situations similar to their own. These needs were clearly not fully satisfied, and this was acknowledged by the plant manager.

The final session of the day was again a department group discussion followed by presentations to the headman in plenary. The groups were asked to discuss two topics: 'advantages and disadvantages of the new organisation', and 'advantages and disadvantages of the corporate philosophy'.

The small group discussions were now more productive, and the groups were able to draw up quite extensive and comprehensive lists within forty-five minutes. The discussions in plenary were lively but lacked the tension and atmosphere of confrontation of the morning sessions. The departmental presentations showed considerable overlap one with another. Whereas in the morning discussions it had been difficult to draw to a conclusion – people wanted to bring in new topics, to argue, to give vent to their feelings, in the final plenary session discussions were more matter of fact. The consensus of the delegates' views were clearly in favour of the changes being made. The advantages of both the restructuring and the corporate philosophy was seen to outweigh the disadvantages. The day finished just after 17.00 hours. The consultant collected the presentations and took them away to summarise them and have them typed up for the following morning.

Even though a number of managers lived within a few miles of the hotel, they had all been invited to stay the night. It was 'expected' that the invitation would be accepted. Most of the managers spent a quiet hour or so in their rooms, and the group reconvened for a drink before dinner at about 19.00 hours.

Dinner was a formal event, the food good and the wine liberally distributed. The liberality with which they were being treated was unexpected by most of the managers. The atmosphere in company X was traditionally quite puritan, the company hospitality towards their managers usually reserved for the annual Christmas event. After dinner the delegates retired to the bar or billiard room. The atmosphere became increasingly convivial and most of the managers stayed up until after midnight. Two got very drunk and one had to be put to bed.

Over breakfast the following morning the conversation focused on the libation of the night before, but at 08.30 prompt the delegates were ready for the second day of the programme.

The first item was to agree on the consultant's summary of the presentations made the previous afternoon. He distributed copies and asked for confirmation that the list reflected their presentations on the advantages and disadvantages of the restructuring and of the new philosophy. There was some discussion. The management group were suspicious that the consultant was manipulating the situation by getting them to commit themselves to a document that could, somehow, be used against them at a later time. Some alterations were made and the list, somewhat grudgingly, accepted. By 09.15 the workshop was able to get down to the main part of the day's programme. Again this involved small group discussions in department teams followed by presentations by each team in plenary. The topic was; 'What problems must we overcome if we are to change our organisation in line with the corporate management philosophy?! Most groups needed between one-and-a-quarter and one-and-a-half hours for their discussions. The presentations took an-hour-and-a-half, and were concluded by lunch time. Again there was considerable overlap among the views of departmental groups, but each also reflected local concerns and matters of interest. The consultant recorded the main points of the presentations and had a document typed ready for distribution and endorsement.

In summary the following areas were perceived as the major problems to be overcome:

1 How do we increase our skills and knowledge to be able to manage effectively within the new organisation?
2 How do we develop personnel systems to complement the new values and the new organisation – particularly in the areas of participation, appraisal and work planning, communications, job evaluation and remuneration including bonus payments?
3 How do we provide training and development for all employees so that they have the knowledge, skills and attitudes to make a

fuller contribution?

4 How do we overcome the problems generated by the break up of the old functional departments?

5 How do we achieve union cooperation?

6 How do we manage the personal problems – feelings of insecurity, reduced opportunities for advancement, resistance to change, inability to cope with the new ways?

7 How do we manage our time more effectively to ensure that we manage long-term and delegate the day-to-day?

8 What information should we be giving to the employees, and how do we communicate this information?

9 How do we measure the changes to ensure that we are becoming more cost effective and productive?

The final afternoon contained two items: establishment of an action plan, and review of the workshop.

Immediately after lunch the management team were asked to review and endorse the consultant's summary of the morning session. This summary, and the summary produced following the previous day's presentations on discussions on the advantages and disadvantages of the corporate management philosophy were the starting point for the afternoon session. The management group were asked to establish what action should be taken to:

1 Ensure that the advantages materialised;
2 Ensure that the disadvantages were overcome;
3 Manage the problems.

They were asked to split up into their small groups, but one of the senior managers asked if that was the best way to go about doing things. He felt that the issues were now sufficiently clear for the larger group to be able to make effective decisions without a great deal of discussion. He also felt that, as any action plan would clearly have to be endorsed by the whole management team, the whole team should be involved in joint planning. These views received some support from other delegates and when the headman intimated that he was quite happy, it was resolved to have the action planning session in plenary.

It soon became apparent that if the discussion focused on action plans to overcome the problems identified in the morning session, they would also incorporate plans to manage the advantages and disadvantages. The management team resolved therefore to concentrate on the problems identified. Discussion was businesslike and productive. As the session continued fewer people made contributions and the contributors were mostly more senior people. However, the managers who remained quiet were attentive, interested, and seemed to endorse the decisions being made. The task was completed rather earlier than anticipated – just in time for tea.

The action proposed was radical and far reaching. It involved major changes in the way people were managed and in union relationships. It involved a great deal of policy and procedure development in a short time. Yet the whole package was put together in a couple of hours and with the endorsement of the whole management group. The plan was, of course yet to be implemented. Ensuring that the plan is implemented is the responsibility of the headman.

By the final session the managers had had enough. They were beginning to feel drained and wanted to go home. The headman took charge and said that he wanted to review the workshop and summarise his feelings. He exposed the flip-chart on which the objectives of the workshop had been listed. The consultant had used this flip-chart on the first morning when explaining the purpose of the workshop. He asked for views on the degree to which these objectives had been achieved. Half-an-hour's lively discussion ensued and the consultant was able to record the following overall assessment and conclusions:

1 The opportunity to discuss the changes that are taking place was beneficial.
2 Managers felt that they had an increasing understanding of:
   (*a*) What the reorganisation was trying to achieve;
   (*b*) The organisation development programme;
   (*c*) The problems that will have to be overcome;
   (*d*) The ways in which these problems can be overcome.
3 The corporate management philosophy was accepted as the basis of the organisation development programme.
4 There was lack of clarity about how the corporate philosophy could be implemented in practice, and concern that without this clarity the change could not be effectively managed.
5 The workshop achieved a spirit in which people worked together as a team.

The headman concluded the workshop. He thanked the managers for their attendance and hard work. He confirmed his view of the workshop as one step in the process of managing the changes needed to make company X more productive and flexible. He committed himself to ensuring that the action plans resulted in real action. He told the management team that he would be agreeing specific objectives with his immediate subordinates. He assured the management team that he intended to keep on with the process of consulting them, and that he would be discussing with the consultant the form and timing of a further workshop in the near future.

The workshop broke up at 16.30.

Appendix 1 provides summaries of the discussions on the 'advantages and disadvantages of the corporate management philosophy' and the 'action plan'.

Workshop principles

The planning workshop described illustrates many of the principles that govern the 'workshop' approach. This section lists those principles. There are thirteen of them.

1 *The headman must define the group's decision making rights*

The ways in which subordinates can become involved in decision making can vary from zero (decisions are imposed) to complete participation (each members of the group has equal influence on decisions being made). No one level of involvement is always right, no one level is always wrong. The headman must decide on what level of involvement is appropriate in any one situation. In company X a number of decisions had been made without consultation with the management group. The organisation restructuring was imposed upon them. The corporate management philosophy was a 'fait accompli'.

The corporate management believed that these were situations where participation and/or consultation would have been inappropriate for the following reasons:

1. The corporate management would not have been willing to consider a different philosophy, so the management team could not influence their decisions.
2. The management team did not have enough information (about future economic trends, company investment plans, Japanese management style, organisation design principles and practices) to make an informed judgement.
3. If the management group had been involved in planning the new structure, they could not have been trusted to make decisions that would benefit the organisation as a whole. Individuals would have been motivated to protect or enhance their own positions and any changes would have tended to reflect the current political status of the managers. Decision making involving all the managers would not have resulted in the revolutionary changes felt necessary by the corporate management.

This illustrates the principle that participation and consultation are not always appropriate, and should not be used when the work group:

1 Are not in a position to influence decisions or cannot change decisions that have already been made;
2 Do not know enough to make effective decisions;
3 Cannot be trusted to make decisions that would be of benefit to the organisation rather than themselves.

The restructuring and the corporate philosophy were therefore imposed. The organisation was operating a 'power' culture: with speed and firmness, but without concern for people's feelings.

Corporate management assumed (in this case quite rightly) that the local management group in company X would accept and implement instructions imposed upon them. They may not like having decisions imposed upon them, but they would conform. If this assumption cannot be made (for instance in a typical 'person' culture) then the imposition of decisions would not be an option open to top management.

The role of the headman was to:

1 Explain the new structures and new philosophy and the reasons for them;
2 Ensure that the management team understood that they were 'non-negotiable';
3 Instruct the management group to implement the change;

and he used the workshop to achieve these objectives.

He avoided 'quasi-consultation' – giving the impression of consulting when in fact no influence over events is possible. He explained through a tape prepared by the managing director and through his own presentation what the restructuring and corporate management philosophy were about.

Just as there are circumstances in which consultation and participation are inappropriate, so there are other circumstances where they should be used, because they generate understanding, trust and commitment. The headman wanted his management group to participate in the decision making wherever this was appropriate. He therefore also made it clear that the implementation of corporate philosophy, and its interpretation within the manager's own area of responsibility, would be managed through a process of consultation and participation. The majority of the workshop was dedicated to that process.

2 *Hold workshops away from the normal workplace*

Going away from the normal workplace is important for two reasons: it ensures that only long-term strategic issues are dealt with, and it gives added status to the process.

If managers are faced with a decision to make about a problem today, and the need to develop a strategic plan for the day-after-tomorrow, today's problem will always take precedent. A workshop requires that people are thinking long-term and that there are no 'today' issues distracting them. Workshop delegates must be insulated from their workplace. A secretary should always be available to take messages. These messages are passed on only at breaktimes (and that includes messages for the 'top brass'). People enjoy being taken away from meetings to deal with problems and decisions about urgent matters back in the factory. It makes them feel important and indispensable. They will therefore encourage their subordinates to contact them; this must be controlled.

Being out of plant also gives the meeting extra status. Somehow the atmosphere is different; it emphasises that the people are involved in a different sort of activity.

3 *Manage the hostility and frustrations and do it early*

The third item on the programme, after the introductions and the managing director's tape, was an invitation to tell the boss what the management team felt about the recent happenings. The objective of this session was to manage the negative feelings. If feelings of anxiety, hostility and frustration exist they have got to be revealed and managed at an early stage. The way to manage them is to expose them openly, and listen to what is being said, following this formula:

1. Invite participants to discuss their feelings amongst themselves in small groups. This will allow them to develop a shared understanding. It will also demonstrate that the feelings each delegate is having are shared by his colleagues and are therefore legitimate, rather than a symptom of disloyalty.
2. Feed back the main points of the group discussion to the whole workshop. This feedback should be by one member of each group, but he should make it clear that he is speaking on behalf of all his colleagues. This session makes public the fact that people have negative feelings but does so in a way that protects the individual. 'I am telling you this only because you ask me to; it is the feeling of all of us'.
3. The headman should listen to what has been said. Telling the boss what you think of him is fun: but it is also dangerous. If the boss wants the feelings to be brought out on the table and dealt with he must create the right atmosphere and then ensure that people are not punished for doing what he has asked. He achieves both of these by practicing good listening skills.

This is usually all that is needed – the opportunity to discuss concerns, to have them defined as legitimate, and to be listened to. The frustrations and anger disappears even if the headman says 'I hear what you say, but there is nothing that can be done'. In the company X planning workshop, the frustration and hostility disappeared just because people were able to express their feelings honestly and openly about having things imposed upon them, and about not being kept informed. They felt they had been listened to. They felt this because the headman showed effective listening skills.

4 *The headman must listen*

Listening skills are not difficult to achieve, and they are critical to good man-management, but they are foreign to the cultures of many of our organisations. The workshop consultant's chief problem at most of the workshops he organises will be to get the headman to listen. But he must do so if the workshop is to be a success. The headman must be briefed beforehand, and usually this has some temporary effect. Within half an hour the first symptom of non-listening will emerge – a 'Yes, but'. Then it gets worse – 'Ah! Now if you knew all the facts, you would not think that way ----', 'I thought that until I had thought it through ----'. Whatever they say, he seems to counter it. The group rapidly loses spontaneity, the old hands keep quiet, the people who continue to press the points get more and more frustrated.

When confronted with a non-listening headman the consultant will try desperately to bring the next coffee break forward.

At the first opportunity the consultant should get the headman in a corner away from the others, the conversation could go something like this:

Consultant:	What do you think of the atmosphere?
Headman:	They don't seem to be as open as you said they would be, I am rather disappointed.
Consultant:	What can you do to make them behave more openly? (by the tone of his voice the consultant is making it clear that he believes that the headman should know the answer).
Headman:	I am not listening, am I?
Consultant:	No, you bloody well are not! Now tell me, how do you listen?

What the headman replies should be something like this:

(a) I am trying to understand what they are thinking and feeling, and my questions will reflect this:

'Tell me more about why you feel that way ----' or 'I don't understand that point, please expand on your thoughts'.

(b) I am not trying to shove my opinions down their throats, and therefore, I will not tell them what my opinions are, unless they specifically ask me for my views.

(c) By a variety of non-verbal clues; eye contact, posture, facial expression, I will demonstrate that whay they are saying is important to me.

(d) I will regularly feed back to them the main points that they are making to show that I have heard and understood.

Consultant: Super. What do you want me to do when you stray?
Headman: You had better give me a firm kick on the ankle.

The effect of the practice of good listening skills by the headman will be rapid and profound. The group will talk more, will become more honest, will relax, will feel they are getting more out of the workshop. They will work through their feelings of hostility, frustration and anger surprisingly quickly.

5 *Provide for their information needs*

In practising good listening skills, the headman will resist providing unsolicited information when he believes that a member of his team has got it wrong, or does not fully understand the background of the situation. But people will have areas of ignorance, and if they are to gain in understanding, these gaps must be filled. The way these information needs are met can be important. The best approach is to set aside a specific time for giving information, and to prepare carefully to ensure that this time is used effectively.

At the company X planning workshop, the consultant took on the role of assembler of items to be addressed at the information session. When he detected that a delegate, or several delegates were unclear about something he would ask the group:

Do you want to know more about -----?'

or

Are you sure you understand the implications of -----?

If the reaction was a general consensus that there was a need for more information or clarification the item was recorded on a flip-chart. At the first session in the afternoon the headman went through the list, doing his best to provide the answers. The advantages of doing it this way are:

(a) A commitment is made to provide for the information needs of the delegates, which reinforces the level of delegate involvement.

(b) The time is utilised effectively and information provided systematically.

(c) The delegates are provided with the answers to the questions they want answered rather than with information the headman wants to give them.

(d) The headman does not have to come out of his listening role in the earlier session.

It is rare for the majority of information needs to be met in the assigned session. The headman does not have all the answers. This is not important. What is important in building up commitment is that the headman is seen as wanting to keep his people informed and wanting to share with them his knowledge. He is seen as wanting to develop in his subordinates a high level of awareness and understanding so that each individual can make a maximum contribution towards managing change.

6 *Don't try to achieve too much, too soon*

The headman sometimes expresses disappointment at the small number of concrete decisions that emerge from a workshop. The action plans are frequently a collection of proposals to set up working parties or study groups; 'John Smith agreed to set up a project group to develop recommendations for an improved communication system' or 'Personnel are asked to put forward a proposal for a revised bonus scheme' or 'The plant manager and the industrial relations manager should inform the union of these discussions'. The headman also frequently expresses concern about the limitations of knowledge shown by many of his managers, and his disappointment that more understanding has not been achieved. The headman is expecting too much from a workshop. Criteria for success should be whether the objectives of the workshop have been met. In the case of our planning workshop the criterion to be used is whether each delegate:

1 Has a better understanding of what the plant manager wants from him;
2 Knows what extra information, knowledge and skill he needs to manage in the new environment;
3 Knows what he has to do;
4 Feels committed to the changes, and to his part within them;
5 Is able to work more effectively as part of a team.

If these criteria have been met the workshop can be judged a success.

Chris Argyris, one of the foremost authorities on organisation development was once blandly asked at a television interview,

Tell me, Professor Argyris, how do you change organisations?

How do you give in a few words an answer to a question to which you have addressed your whole career? Argyris sighed and then responded:

Slowly.

This is probably the best brief answer that can be given. Organisation change takes time. The planning workshop in company X was designed to lay a foundation on which to build an organisation development programme that would last for five years. The success of the overall programme would provide the answer to questions on how firmly the foundations were laid.

8 *Get them to think it through for themselves*

The planning workshop in our case history includes very little time in which information was being presented in a formal way. The introduction, the managing director's tape and the concluding session could be described as formal presentations. The information giving session by the headman was semi-formal and semi-structured. During the rest of the time, some 75 per cent of the total, the participants were the ones who did all the work. The role of the consultant was not to provide the delegates with material from which they can learn, but to provide a framework within which they can learn from each other.

Adults, particularly adults whose environment involves a great deal of uncertainty, do not take information on trust. They evaluate new information against their own data base – their experience. They ask questions: Does it make sense?, Will it work?

They also evaluate new information or concepts on a political dimension: Will my boss go along with it? Will my subordinates feel threatened? Will my colleagues be hostile?

It is for these reasons that it is critical that a group of organisation members are given the opportunity to evaluate both the 'will it work' and 'is it acceptable' dimensions. They do this best through a process of exploring new ideas, information and concepts with their peers in an atmosphere where nothing inhibits the free discussion of the topics. That is why small group discussions take so large a percentage of the time. Small groups encourage contributions from everyone, large groups encourage contributions only from opinion leaders. In our case study the delegates had discussions within their normal work groups. The headman was not invited, and therefore they felt more free to be open and frank, and more able to learn from one another.

9 *Use a problem solving approach*

One of the ways to assess the culture of an organisation is to listen carefully to the words people use when they are evaluating their colleagues. Do they assess them in terms of positive achievements:

> Each time he has taken over a market area, the overall sales figures have improved . . . .
>
> or
>
> The people in his department always seem highly motivated . . . .?

Or on the other hand do they assess people on the bricks they have dropped?

> He was the one who mistook the visiting Professor for a waiter and ordered him to fetch some sandwiches . . . .

There are major differences between organisations on this dimension of positive and negative evaluation, and it is important. If you are evaluated on the basis of the clangers you drop, then the best way to ensure a high evaluation is to avoid any risky action. If you do nothing, you cannot make any mistakes. If, on the other hand you are evaluated on your achievements against targets or objectives then you are motivated to search for better ways of doing things: you are more likely to use a problem solving approach.

In order to encourage a problem solving approach in an organisation, having problems must be seen as legitimate. Only if problems are brought into the open can the organisation's efforts be directed towards solving them. If people are evaluated on the basis of their not having problems or not giving their boss problems, they will be motivated to hide them. If problems are not surfaced, they cannot be solved so individuals will not improve their standard of performance and the organisation cannot become more effective.

It is the management's role to ensure an atmosphere of trust where organisation members are rewarded for being open and surfacing the problems they are having.

At our workshop the identification and managing of problems is a key task. Specific sessions are assigned to problem identification and action planning. The success of these sessions depends upon the creation of an atmosphere where people are willing to reveal the issues. This atmosphere is not difficult to produce, but it is easy to destroy. Again the role of the headman is critical. He must reward, by reinforcement and encouragement, problem solving activities. He must avoid the negative remarks:

> For Heaven's sake! I thought we had sorted that one out
> last spring . . . . . .

The consultant or catalyst also should play a role by identifying the participants whose approach is essentially negative and working with them to modify their behaviour.

10 *Build teams*

A workshop involves a group of people working together. The success of the workshop depends upon the capacity of those people to work together effectively. They need to ensure that each individual's contribution is utilised; they must trust each other sufficiently to be open and honest in their discussions. The workshop must be organised in a way that encourages the growth of a team spirit and therefore of effective interpersonal relationships.

The small group discussions held during the company X planning workshop took place in the normal work group and were essentially team building activities.

The tasks allocated to the group were successfully completed and the people felt more confident and personally satisfied because they had participated in successful group activities. The social evening also can have an important effect in building a team spirit particularly if the organisation does not usually indulge its members in this way.

The role of the consultant can be crucial. He should be a 'process' specialist, (knowledgeable and experienced in group dynamics). As an expert and an outsider he is in an ideal situation to observe what is happening within each group and propose action where necessary to improve team effectiveness. During the workshop, he should pay occasional visits to each work group, observing the way the group operates and offering advice, where necessary, on how the process of decision making and consensus forming can be made more effective.

11 *Be flexible*

Flexibility is required in both the planning and the managing of a workshop. Workshops never go according to plan. No matter how carefully the programme is planned in advance something always happens that requires changes to be made. In our planning workship, the participants decided that they wanted to deal with the action plan on the final afternoon in a plenary session. The fact that the workshop takes on a life of its own is a sign of its health and virility. It is important that the changing needs are reacted to flexibly.

The consultant's job is to assess the mood and needs of the group participants and advise the headman of any changes that are necessary.

12 *Action plan*

One of the main purposes of having a workshop is to develop an action plan. The action plan is developed through two activities.

1. The discussions are recorded and summarised. In the company X workshop the summaries were of two main discussion topics:
   (*a*) The advantages and disadvantages of change;
   (*b*) The problems to be managed to facilitate change.
   When these summaries have been endorsed, they become the foundation for the second activity.
2. The participants list what should be done to:
   (*a*) Grasp the opportunities provided by the advantages;
   (*b*) Reduce the potential damage of the disadvantages;
   (*c*) Solve the problems.

One of the most likely causes of limited success of a workshop activity relates to the action plans. The problem is not in the production of the plans – that invariably happens. What is vital is to ensure that the plans are implemented successfully. That is the headman's role.

13 *Start at the top*

This organisation development programme is based on the principle that change at the top must occur before changes at the lower level of the organisation can be introduced successfully. Once the top levels are ready to manage change, the programme should systematically involve the next level down. This 'cascade down' approach to organisation development is discussed in greater detail in Chapter Seven.

The role of the headman

Some organisations seem to work quite well despite the top management. In some organisations the top management seem to have little real influence on what goes on. However, organisation change is the responsibility of top management, so in all workshops the influence of the headman will be of paramount importance. He must understand and agree his role, and he must play it effectively. Workshops are about organisational change, and aiding the organisation adjust to its environment. The headman, as the most senior organisation member, should manage with the longest time scale. His job should not be about the day-to-day, but about visions of the future, environmental scanning, providing a lead and a direction, and that includes decisions about how to manage change. Workshops are therefore, essentially to help the headman achieve his job objectives.

The headman's tasks and roles at the workshop are different from those of the other participants.

1 He decides on whether or not to use a participatory workshop approach. He listens to advice on the advantages and costs of such an approach; and to advice on the circumstances in which a workshop should be used, and on those where alternatives are more appropriate. He then makes his decision.
2 He agrees on the programme objectives and content.
3 He sets the scene in his introduction, by explaining the purpose of the workshop, his belief in managing change through involvement and the importance of the exercise in which the people are involved. He will also make clear what are 'givens': those areas which will not involve consultation and participation.
4 During the workshop he practises listening skills; he also helps create a problem solving and team building atmosphere by insisting that the participants think things through, by rewarding activities that identify problems and by encouraging people to work together.
5 He emphasises the development of an action plan; he commits himself to implement the plans, he meets this commitment.

The problems are most likely to lie in items 4 and 5. It is difficult for many headmen to take what appears to be a passive role; particularly when they disagree with what is being said. It is also difficult to give priority to implementing long-term action plans when today's problems are so pressing. The headman must have a clear understanding of the problems and pitfalls implicit in the route he is planning to follow before he embarks on the workshop path. He must understand the benefits that the workshop approach will bring in generating the committed organisation. He must also understand that the process is a long and hard one, with many short-term disadvantages.

Summary and conclusions

The main points made in this chapter can be summarised as follows:

1 A workshop is a gathering of the members of a work team where all participate in developing and implementing plans for the future. A workshop can be held for work teams in any level of an organisation.
2 The workshop approach is based on the assumption that the talents of all the organisation members will be fully utilised only if an organisation follows, over many years, policies that lead to

increased understanding, improved communications, involvement of people in decision making, teamwork development and well defined authorities and responsibilities. If such policies are followed then a culture will be developed whose principal characteristic is worker commitment.

3 The workshop approach will bring about both planned organisation change and the development of this committed organisation culture.

4 Alternatively, more authoritarian approaches, can be successfully used to induce organisation change. Sometimes these authoritarian approaches are necessary, but they will inhibit the development of a committed culture.

5 The planning workshop in company X began the planning by management by an organisation development programme. The workshop was described in order to illustrate the techniques that are used for maximising understanding, increasing commitment and changing attitudes, and the principles implicit in effective workshop activities.

6 These principles are:
(*a*) The areas where the group has the rights and responsibilities to make decisions must be defined;
(*b*) The focus should be on long-term planning and developing a 'vision' of the future;
(*c*) Hostilities and frustrations must be confronted and managed;
(*d*) The workshop leader must demonstrate a participatory management style, and show listening skills;
(*e*) Information needs must be met;
(*f*) The workshop members must be allowed to think through the issues they consider important, and at a pace with which they feel comfortable;
(*g*) The programme should facilitate team building, problem solving and action planning;
(*h*) Change must start at the top.

7 The role of the most senior manager in establishing the workshop approach is crucial. He must decide that the approach is appropriate, behave in conformity with the principles, commit himself to implement the action plans, and accept the short-term difficulties of managing in a way which maximises long-term advantages.

The planning workshop described in this chapter is the first of many that must take place during the organisation development programme. Therefore the workshop approach requires a number of years of organisation stability to produce the committed culture. This approach would be inappropriate for managing change in a crisis situation. Crisis can be produced by an unpredictable and far reaching change in the environment within which the organisation operates (e.g. cutting off of raw materials because of political action in a supplier country). But a crisis can also steal up on an organisation because of its past inability to make on-going adjustments to a normally changing environment until change is forced upon it.

Many organisations find themselves in a crisis situation because they have been unable or unwilling to react appropriately to changes in the environment in which they operate. An organisation that has developed a culture based on consultation, participation, involvement and communications will develop employees who are committed to working together to identify and solve problems they are having at work, and to finding better ways of doing things. Such an organisation will not find itself having to face such major crisis situations because it will have had the ability to continuously adjust to changes in its environment, no matter whether those changes are political, economic, social, commercial or technical. One of the long-term objectives of the organisation development programme is to produce such an organisation.

6 Developing the Guidelines

The planning workshop was held in order to lay the foundations for the organisation development programme. The plant manager knew that much more work with his management group was necessary before the time would be right to attempt change in other parts of the organisation. He believed that the management should think more about the way they managed their subordinates, and he believed that a systematic set of principles were needed to guide the action programme.

The plant manager had a clear idea of the approaches to manmanagement he wanted adopted in company X. He believed that a consulting and participatory style and the systematic involvement of all organisation members in making decisions about their own working environment would lead, in time, to an increase in commitment by all to work together to maximise the organisation's effectiveness.

In such organisations the management will delegate authority and responsibility; they will believe that all employees have a potential for making a contribution; they will listen to and where possible implement suggestions and proposals developed at the lower levels.

The plant manager also believed the converse to be true: an organisation whose management style is traditional, 'scientific' and authoritarian will have a workforce that is uncommitted and uncooperative. For someone who believes that in the highly competitive conditions of the 1980s, his organisation will thrive only if it can match the competition by utilising all its human resources effectively the problem is this: How can he change the beliefs and attitudes of his management away from the traditional ways they have learned during their years as practising managers, towards an approach closer to that which the Japanese seem to find so successful? To the plant manager this was the next critical question because he believed that the changing of an organisational culture can only occur if the change begins at the top: with himself and his top management team. The next workshop was designed to tackle this problem.

At the planning workshop the corporate management philosophy was expounded. The management team was asked to consider this philosophy and to say what they thought about it. The company X management team accepted, in general terms, the corporate management philosophy. However, they still had reservations, particularly about how it could be turned into practical day-to-day management techniques. It was also clear that many of the managers did not fully understand the corporate philosophy. At the end of the workshop the headman assured the team that he intended to keep up the consultation process, and that he would be discussing with the consultant the form and timing of a further workshop in the near future. He asked the consultant to talk to the managers about their feelings and about their views on the next step. Almost without exception their concern was with understanding and implementing the corporate management philosophy. The consultant discussed this with the headman and he agreed that the next workshop should aim to increase the managers' knowledge.

However, the headman had additional objectives for this second workshop. He wanted his management team to actively work towards establishing the principles that they believed should be the basis of the future approach to people management. Only if they developed the principles would they be fully committed to them. The principles, once established could easily be translated into a set of guidelines that would become an agreed basis for action to implement the organisation development programme in company X. These guidelines would be a reflection of the manager's understanding of how best to apply practically the corporate management philosophy in company X. This workshop, therefore became known as the management principles workshop, and it resulted in a set of guidelines to be used to stimulate and coordinate the organisation development programme.

In summary the objectives of the management principles workshop were:

1 To increase understanding of practical management techniques which are examples of applications of the corporate management philosophy.
2 To review which of these techniques and approaches have practical applications for, and are relevant to, improving the effectiveness of company X.

3 To agree a set of principles that will provide guidelines for future organisation development.

The workshop programme

The date was set for some six weeks ahead and again all the managers were invited. It was estimated that one-and-a-half days would be needed for this workshop. The headman felt that it was unnecessary to hire the local hotel or to stay the night. It was agreed, however, that the workshop should take place out of plant.

The headman introduced the workshop. He emphasised that the corporate management philosophy was a series of broad concepts that appeared to be endorsed by the management team. Within these concepts it was up to the team to learn more about the alternative approaches to the management of human resources, and to collectively extract from this learning, the things which make sense to them and to reject those things which they felt did not fit into company X history and traditions.

After this introduction the first day of the workshop consisted of a number of presentations. These presentations were either by experienced 'experts', or were films designed to illustrate different management techniques. These presentations were:

1 Flagtown: Description of plant within the corporation that had operated the corporate management philosophy since it began operations on a green field site.
2 Job redesign: Practical applications presented by a consultant who had advised on the projects.
3 Job rotation and job enrichment: Film material designed for management training.
4 Japanese management style: A presentation encompassing much the same ground as Chapter Three.

After each presentation, the management team were asked two questions:

1 What aspects of what you have seen and heard do you feel should be incorporated in the way we do things here?
2 What aspects of what you have seen and heard do you feel should be avoided?

The results of the discussions were recorded on two flip-charts: one of the 'do's' one for the 'don'ts'. The day was concluded with a recap. of the corporate management philosophy tape which the managing director had recorded, and which had been used to introduce the concepts at the planning workshop. The consultant took the flip-charts away and worked overtime to get the main points down on paper for the next morning.

The agenda for day two consisted of two items: to ratify the consultant's summary of do's and don'ts, and to decide what action should be taken as a result of the learning.

Forty-five minutes were spent in plenary going through and agreeing the document the consultant had produced. The summary reflected the fact that the presentations had covered a great deal of different ground and that the discussions had been lively and the manager's responses generally positive. It covered decision making and delegation, security, involvement, training, monitoring, job redesign, autonomy, role of specialists, role of supervision, communications and union relations.

The managers were then asked to work in their department groups. They were asked to discuss the now-agreed list, to decide if the list represented guidelines for future management action to which they were willing to commit themselves. They needed about one hour for this discussion, and by mid-morning the workshop was able to be reconvened for a plenary session.

It became clear when the discussions started that the different departmental teams had come to similar conclusions. Each was prepared to endorse the summary with some minor modifications, but they each felt the way change was introduced, and the speed of implementing change should be clarified. They were afraid that their endorsement of the list would lead to pressures to make inappropriate changes too rapidly. They felt that they should not be making change for change's sake, but because they believed that the changes would lead to long-term improvements in productivity, quality, costs and flexibility. The management said that they felt they were in danger of being railroaded. They still felt that they were being pushed along a route they did not fully understand and where the outcomes were uncertain. They felt they were putting themselves at risk. The headman listened to their reservations sympathetically. The management said that they would like these concerns 'built into' the summary (we were now calling the summary 'the guidelines') and when the headman readily agreed to this the consultant was given the job of redrafting. The final set of guidelines was then accepted by the team and is presented in full in Appendix Two.

Workshop outcome

The headman was delighted. He had achieved a document which listed, in detail, the management approach and action needed to transform the organisation. The document had been produced by the management team, and he had every reason to believe they were committed to it. Now that he had the guidelines, the achievement of the changes the headman was looking for would now require two things: time, and his continuing commitment.

The success of the workshop in achieving significant changes in management attitudes towards using a more consulting and participatory style was due to the managers being given the opportunity to increase their understanding, and the opportunity to work through the information they had received so that they could make decisions on what made sense to them. The result was not only a comprehensive and relevant list of management principles (the consultant could have produced such a list), but more importantly, a commitment to those principles and to action to implement them. The management team had taken a set of general principles (the corporate management philosophy) and had worked through how these general principles could be applied in detail in their specific organisation.

The management principles workshop is an essential stage in the organisation development process. The next logical stage will normally become clear towards the end of the workshop. Usually the next questions are:

> Now that we have our guidelines, and now that we feel committed to the values the guidelines contain, how do we go about actually doing something?
> Who is going to develop proposals, how are these proposals going to be legitimised?
> How are we going to involve the unions?
> What time scale are we going to have?
> Where do we begin?

The management team need to agree answers to these questions, and others. The headman will be clear that another day needs to be allocated to a further workshop, once the dust has settled on the current one.

Summary and conclusions

The planning workshop should be followed by a further workshop to increase the management knowledge about, and commitment to, practical applications of the corporate management philosophy. One concrete outcome of this second workshop should be a set of guidelines to stimulate and coordinate the organisation development programme.

Further work with management will be needed to plan the logistics of the organisation development programme, but the stage has now been reached where other organisation members should become involved. Chapter Eight describes the 'cascade down' process which is designed to progressively increase the involvement in and influence over, the organisation development programme, by the lower levels of the organisation.

7 The Cascading Workshop Programme

More than six months has now passed since the plant manager agreed an organisation development plan for company X with the managing director. During this period progress has been made in a number of areas:

1 A major restructuring had been announced and implemented, with most managers having new responsibilities.
2 A management planning workshop had been held which laid down the foundation for the organisation development programme.
3 A management principles workshop had been held to increase management's understanding of the organisation development programme and to create a set of guidelines within which the progress of the programme would be coordinated.

It is now time to involve other members of the organisation.

The workshop approach implies a 'cascade down' process of organisation change. According to this process, change must begin at the highest levels in the organisation because it is management's role to determine the values and principles that are to be used, and because the management must make change happen. Their understanding, commitment and action must be the starting point. Once this foundation has been laid a process of involving other organisation members in the changes that affect their working environment can begin.

The systematic involvement in change of all organisation members is important for two main reasons:

1 Consulting and participating with people in the decisions that affect their day-to-day working environment builds feelings of commitment to the organisation's objectives.
2 The 'cascade down' approach requires that each member of the organisation with managerial or supervisory responsibility accepts that it is his job to manage the change programme within his area of responsibility. The department manager takes on the responsibility for the organisation development programme within his department. His middle managers and supervisors take on the detailed planning for organisation change, and, once they are agreed, take responsibility for implementing those plans. It is therefore crucial to this process that organisation members below management level understand and are committed to the programme, and are able to train and motivate the people for whose performance they are responsible.

In this chapter workshops are described for three key groups of employees:

1 Supervision: those who directly manage the people who 'do' (referred to in this chapter as 'operators') and who ultimately must be responsible for bringing about changes in the way operators are managed so that their talents are fully utilised.
2 Specialists: those people who use their skills and knowledge to support the supervisors and operators.
3 Operators: who may be highly skilled, highly trained and highly paid, but are ultimately the 'doers'. Shopfloor machine operators, clerks, computer programmers, assemblers, salesmen all fit into this category; their distinguishing characteristic is that they have the responsibility for directly achieving something themselves, whether it is a machined part, an invoice, an assembly, contract or a computer programme. The operators do not support, manage or supervise; they directly produce the goods and services.

Workshops with all three groups are necessary for successful organisation change. Supervision must acquire the necessary knowledge so that they understand the reasons for, and the principles behind, the new ways of working; they must have the right supportive attitudes towards the change; and they must themselves learn to manage their subordinates in a way that supports the change. Specialist support staff will take on a different relationship to other organisation members as the organisation development programme proceeds. They must acquire new knowledge, attitudes and behaviour.

The operator workshop represents the final stage in the 'cascade down' process. They follow workshops with management, supervision and specialists because organisation development at one level can only be achieved if preceded by organisation development at the level above. But when the organisation is able to change the way the jobs are organised at the operator level, and when all organisation members feel that they are involved in decision making within those areas that directly affect them then there will also be a workforce of growing commitment and an organisation more and more capable of adjusting rapidly and effectively to changes in its external environment.

Supervisor workshops

Objectives

At the beginning of the organisation development programme in company X the management group had felt hostility towards both corporate management and their own plant manager. They had felt they had not been kept informed, and they had not been consulted. One of the objects of the management planning workshop was to manage these hostile feelings by informing, listening, consulting and making it clear that future changes, as long as there was conformity to the overall corporate strategy, would fully involve managers in planning and implementing the changes. After the workshop the managers felt better: they had a better understanding of what was happening, they felt they were being involved, they had a clearer idea of what was expected of them. They did not feel fully comfortable however until after the second workshop at which they learned more about relevant management techniques and where they developed the management principles. It was then the turn of their subordinates to feel uncomfortable. They were now feeling that changes were being imposed upon them. Senior management were now condemned as not informing and not consulting.

Under the 'cascade down' process, once the management feel they understand what is going on, and feel committed to the changes taking place, it is time to involve the next level down – normally in a large manufacturing plant, the junior management or supervisory level.

This involvement should begin with a workshop. This workshop should have many similarities with the planning workshop attended by management, and should incorporate some of the learning activities that were the foundation of the management principles workshop. This will help integrate the overall process of organisation change and organisation development. The objectives of the supervisor workshop will be the same as the objectives of the first management workshop:

to inform, involve, and build commitment. For company X these objectives can be identified more specifically as follows:

1 To inform supervision of:
   (*a*) Corporate management philosophy, and the reasons for the organisation development programme;
   (*b*) Progress of the organisation development programme to date.
2 To increase understanding of the models of human resource management used by management to develop the management principles.
3 To provide an opportunity for consultation with supervision on the corporate management philosophy and the organisation development programme.

Programme

This is an important workshop and should be recognised as such. Two days will be needed. The workshop should be residential as this will show that the organisation believes that the supervisory group has an important role to play in implementing the organisation development programme. A senior manager should take the headman's role and middle management should attend. There will be a need to record discussions and presentations and a scribe (who may be a manager) is useful. The headman's boss should give the introduction to emphasise his commitment.

The supervisor workshop programme at company X consisted of three types of sessions:

1 Information giving – at which workshop members were informed about corporate management philosophy, its origins and philosophy, and progress in implementing the organisation development programme to date. This information was given out early in the programme as it provided the basis of later discussions. The tape of the managing director talking about the corporate management philosophy was used for the opening session, and this was followed by a presentation on what had happened so far and included:
   (*a*) The decisions already taken by management about action needed and principles to be followed. These decisions became 'the givens' for the supervision.
   (*b*) The events that had occurred in the organisation development programme about which the supervisors needed to know, together with an explanation of the reasons for these changes (e.g. changes in organisation structures,

progress of working parties considering ways of improving the communication system).

The headman did not encourage discussion during these sessions, although he did answer specific questions.

2 Examples of the corporate management philosophy in practice – these sessions were provided in order to increase the supervisor's knowledge of what can be done and what is being done elsewhere. This knowledge allowed them to understand the principles developed by their own management more easily.

3 Discussions using the small group – plenary techniques. These discussions were designed to allow consultation with supervision on the organisation development programme. The first session was in addition designed to expose and manage any hostilities and frustrations felt by the group (and there were some). As always this was a key part of the programme and had to be managed effectively in line with the principles laid out in Chapter Five. The rest of the consultation session asked the supervisors to inform management about their views on:

(*a*) Advantages and disadvantages of the organisation development programme for supervision;

(*b*) Action that should be taken to implement the programme by:

(*i*) senior management

(*ii*) department management

(*iii*) supervision

These sessions ensured that the supervisory views were listened to by management. Records of the presentations also formed the basis of active consultation with supervision after the workshop programme was completed.

Outcome

It is important that the supervisors are not only listened to, but their views actively taken into consideration. The presentations made by the supervisors to the management observing the workshop in company X were used as a basis for action planning. A summary of the views expressed at a number of different workshops was prepared and reviewed as follows:

1 Senior management considered the supervisor's views on what they (the senior management) should be doing to support the implementation of the organisation development programme and responded with commitment to action or an explanation of why no action would be taken.

2 Department managers met with their middle managers to consider and respond to the views of supervisors on what they (middle management) should be doing.
3 The supervisors met after the workshops in their own department groups to identify the action they would take.

The main points of the workshop presentations, together with the action responses to them, are given in full in Appendix Three.

One of the unplanned, but nevertheless important outcomes of supervisor workshops is that management learn things they did not know before. They will gain a much clearer idea of the way supervisors see their world, and also an increased understanding about many other things that are happening at work. This learning on the management's part will, of course, only take place if they are using their listening skills effectively.

Another unplanned, but highly beneficial outcome of a well run workshop is improved personal relations between management and supervision. Simply by having a workshop attended by management and supervision out of plant, the management are practicing the Japanese approach of spending some of their spare time with colleagues at different levels, in social and recreational activities.

A workshop for specialist support staff

Objectives

Chapters Four and Ten discuss the changes in organisational structures that can facilitate organisation development. One of the themes developed in these chapters is that change is facilitated if the specialist support staff are organised so that they become part of an operational team, rather than a member of a large functional department. Such teams lead to better cooperation between functions, better communications, more individual development, more flexibility, more emphasis on the central tasks of the organisation, and more job satisfaction. In this type of structure skills and knowledge of the specialist becomes more effectively directed. One of the effects of such organisation restructuring is that the specialist must become more versatile. Instead of an approach to his job based on 'I have the skill, I will use that skill as and when it is needed', he needs to think 'There are skilled jobs to be done within my team, I must develop all the skills necessary to do those jobs and so support the team of which I am a member'.

Gaining the acceptance of specialists to such changes can be difficult: they represent a major upheaval in the specialist's working routines. Instructions issued in an authoritarian way are likely to lead to feelings of insecurity and hostility, and to obstructive and unco-operative behaviour. It may well be possible for management to impose the change. Qualified specialist support staff are often more willing to accept decisions imposed upon them by authoritarian management, than are other work groups. The imposition of change by management dictate would, however, inhibit the process of building commitment of these key employees to the new way of working. It would not facilitate the integration of the specialist into a work team, and therefore, would not be making best use of the talents the specialist has to offer. The aim of the workshop approach is the achievement of this commitment, and the effective use of the skills and talents of all the people.

This section describes a workshop in company X. The management team have completed their planning workshop and their management principles workshop. Resulting from these workshops, management have decided to restructure the support services, so that they become more integrated with the manufacturing process. A middle manager has been delegated to draw up plans for the reorganisation of engineering services. A process of consultation has been completed and the plans endorsed by senior management. It is now time to invite the engineers to a workshop whose objectives are:

1. To inform about the organisation development programme, and the reasons for it.
2. To inform about the plans to implement the programme with the engineering function.
3. To consult on these plans.
4. To establish action plans for future action.

Programme

The headman for this workshop was the middle manager who prepared the plans for the reorganisation of the function. The workshop lasted one day, and took place away from the plant. This gave the workshop status and minimised the interruptions. All the engineers were invited.

The first part of the programme was directed towards satisfying the workshop member's information needs. Before the workshop the members knew that change was in the air, but little else. They were not familiar with the management philosophy or management principles which were driving the changes. The philosophy and the principles must be understood if the reasons for the changes in the way the specialist work is organised are to be appreciated. The headman therefore, initially made a presentation which informed the workshop members of the thinking behind the organisation development programme, and the events that had occurred to date. He used visual aids that the training department had created for him. He answered questions but at this stage did not encourage discussion.

During the next stage of the workshop the headman explained his plan for applying the philosophy and the principles within the function. He made it clear what the 'givens', were, where he wished to consult with the specialists, and where he would accept the group's decision on what was to happen. He explained that the movement from the organisation of specialists in functional departments to the organisation of specialists in support teams was a 'given' as was the despecialising of jobs. The headman said he was willing to consult on the allocation of individuals to different teams, but reserved the right to make the final decision. He emphasised that he wished to involve the workshop members, as much as possible, and therefore he would be setting up project groups to plan the details of the changes. The headman saw himself as providing a framework within which the workshop members could provide the detailed action plan. His presentation included a concrete example of the new way of working in practice. The headman answered questions but once again did not encourage discussion.

These two presentations took the programme to a break for coffee. The atmosphere was brittle. People were standing around in conspiratorial groups. The headman did not feel comfortable. After coffee it was time for the next crucial stage. The hostilities had to be confronted and managed.

Major changes, and particularly changes where the people involved feel things are being imposed upon them and where they feel they do not fully understand what is going on and why, invariably lead to feelings of frustration and hostility. If the people have traditionally been treated as different and more privileged than other employees there will be status concerns to manage. This workshop, of all those described in this book is the most likely to be faced with hostile reactions from the members. Of all the groups, the specialists face the greatest changes: in job content, in role relationships and in status during an organisation development programme.

The headman kept clearly in mind the rules for handling hostility and frustration described in Chapter Five:

1 The members should have the opportunity to discuss their feelings in small groups.
2 The feelings of the members should be communicated by a spokesman to the headman at a plenary session.
3 The headman must listen, and by his behaviour show that the feelings that the people are having are understandable, and not taken by him as signifying disloyalty.
4 The headman must emphasise his commitment, within the

'givens' to the involvement of all the workshop members in planning the change and implementing the programme.

5 The headman should listen to any 'hardship cases', and undertake to review them with the individuals concerned. (These 'hardship cases' are usually long serving, older employees who do not feel able to change. The organisation should attempt to be sufficiently flexible to accommodate these people's needs. If the group defined the problem, there will be no accusations of unfair or privileged treatment for these individuals).

He followed these rules during the rest of the morning, and invited the workshop members to form groups to discuss the advantages and disadvantages of the programme, and their personal concerns with it. He listened carefully and sympathetically to the presentations made by a spokesman for each group at a plenary session and he soon found that the emotional tension was draining away.

Whilst the feelings of hostility tend to be highest in specialist workshops, they also tend to be easiest to manage. This group is more likely than their supervisor or operator colleagues to understand and appreciate the reasons for change, welcome the opportunity for involvement, welcome the opportunity for wider and different jobs and relationships, and appreciate working for an organisation with a clear idea of where it is going and how it is getting there.

The atmosphere at lunch was very different from the atmosphere at coffee. People felt they had 'got it off their chests' and there was something exhilarating about telling the boss what you think about him and apparently getting away with it. There was a lot of talk, most of it reflecting forward thinking.

The afternoon session concentrated on problem identification and action planning using small group discussions – report back process. The topics for discussion were:

1 Identification of problems to be overcome to implement the organisation development programme within the function.
2 Identification of action needed to implement the programme.
3 Development of plans to overcome the problems and ensure appropriate action.

The main points of the presentations were recorded and used by the headman as follow-up action plans. The afternoon session felt rather flat; all the emotion had been expended during the morning.

Outcome

Too much in the way of concrete plans or decisions should not be expected to emerge at a specialist workshop. If, at the end of the day, the workshop members understand more clearly the management philosophy and what the organisation development programme is all about, have a clearer idea of what their involvement in managing the change programme will be, have a clearer idea of their future work role, and have mapped out an outline of the action that needs to be taken to implement change, then the workshop will have been a success. It is up to the headman to take the outline action plans and ensure progress in the implementation of the new way of working during the following months.

Appendix Four presents a summary of the presentations made at the engineers' 'changing support staff' workshop in company X. The same sort of material would be generated at a workshop for any work group of specialists (e.g. accountants, production controllers, buyers, trainers, personnel officers, quality engineers) whose jobs are to be widened (and therefore despecialised). The sort of response would be the same, and many of the concerns raised by the engineers in this example would be felt by any other specialist group in the same situation.

Operator workshops

Objectives

The final workshop described in this chapter is for the 'doers', called here operators. The term 'operator' is used to refer to the people who operate a process or procedure, as opposed to those who manage, supervise, support or advise. The operators may be involved in a great variety of tasks in a large organisation: machining, assembly, clerical work, selling, programming computers. They all have one thing in common: they are the organisation's 'doers'.

The operator workshop takes place when the organisation culture has changed sufficiently, through the organisation development programme, to support changes at the operator level. The reorganisation or redesign of operator work should not take place until management, supervision and support staff understand what is going on, and are willing and able to change their approach to their work in order to facilitate changes in operator jobs.

Changes to the 'doers' tasks are usually given fairly specific titles: job enrichment, job redesign, job enlargement, job rotation. Changes to the way they interact with their colleagues and supervision and the way their work is assigned and organised come under the heading of autonomous or semi-autonomous work groups. Systems for involving operators in decision making and action planning are often referred to as quality circles, but different organisations use different terminology.

The precise way in which this workshop should be run will depend on many factors, but especially the educational background and level of intelligence of the work group and the history of involvement of the work group in decision making. Groups of computer programmers or salesmen are more likely to be better educated than machine operators, and they are more likely to have been managed in a non-authoritarian way (although this will certainly not always be the case). If the work group is bright, well educated and used to being consulted, then an operator workshop would concentrate on providing information about the organisation development programme and beginning the consultation process. The workshop described in this section would not be necessary for such a work group. Work groups whose members are less well educated, and who have been the victims over many years of authoritarian management style which typifies so much of Western manufacturing industry, would need to be involved in activities to increase trust and skill before they would be able or willing to become involved in major changes in the way their work is organised.

The workshop programme described in this section was designed for such a shopfloor operator group in company X. The work group members varied in their capabilities, many of them were conservative (in the sense of against change), many of them had some distrust of management, many felt that management treated them as extensions to their machines and all felt that the company did not keep them informed on what was going on. At the same time these same group members would be offended if it was suggested that they were not commited to, and loyal to the company. They also wanted to know what the union's reaction to these novel events was, and were very anxious not to find themselves being used as a football to be kicked around during a union-management conflict.

The workshop designed for such a group must have different characteristics from workshops designed for managers, supervisors, or specialists. They must take into account the different abilities and experiences of the prospective workshop members. The main differences are as follows:

1 The pace must be slower; to accommodate the slower pace of learning of some work group members but more importantly to ensure that the work group does not feel railroaded.
2 The group must have a sheltered introduction to involvement, by being given the opportunity for realistic consultation in an area where they have some knowledge, interest, and competence.
3 Management would initially have to do the creative thinking, at least until the problem solving capacity (and trust) of the group

had been built up. However, although management would take the lead, involvement of the group members in planning and action to implement plans would be encouraged wherever this was possible.

4 Because of higher levels of mistrust, management would have to demonstrate their willingness to listen to problems, to give the problems priority, and support the implementation of action for improvements before operators would begin to feel prepared to change their behaviour. The more management can demonstrate this, the more they will build trust, and the more the work group will take a more positive view of proposals for major changes in the way they have normally operated.

5 The union must at best be neutral and ideally supportive. Consultative or participatory changes are not possible if the union is hostile. (See Chapter Nine for a discussion of union involvement in organisation development.)

6 Discussion sessions would need to be more structured and shorter. Operator groups in conventionally run organisations are less willing to be open than supervisors or managers, because they feel less self-confident and less able to contribute to discussions. It takes time to build confidence, competence and trust, and therefore, to develop the capacity to contribute towards increasing the work group's effectiveness.

7 Presentations would need to be simpler, and more professional. Operator groups will, even less than management and supervision, be willing to sit and listen. They will react strongly to any process they see as talking down to them, but at the same time many will have difficulty understanding the concepts.

8 Presentations should be more parochial. Operator work groups will be less interested in the overall strategies than in the things that are going to affect their day-to-day activities. Presentations must concentrate on the things that have immediate effect on the operator's working environment.

Programme

Our company X operator workshop was designed to take account of the differences outlined above. The workshop had two separate stages.

Stage One

Stage one was a series of sessions whose objectives were to involve the operator in doing something to improve the way his work group performs through identifying problems and taking action to solve the problems. This stage gave the operators preliminary practice in involvement in a 'sheltered' situation and began the process of building (however slowly) competence and trust. It also allowed management to be seen as listening and supportive. There were three sessions in stage one. Each session took about two hours and was attended by all the operators in the work group with their supervisor, who acted as headman.

The first session was a brainstorming on the subject of 'Things that can be done to make this unit more effective and to increase job satisfaction'. The results of the brainstorming was taken by the headman to his departmental manager, and they jointly developed plans to put some of the suggestions into practice.

The second session took place a week later and was attended by the departmental manager (by invitation). The headman put the action plan to the workshop members. Priorities were set, and the people responsible for getting things done (including volunteer operators) were identified.

The third session took place three months later, and reviewed the progress of the plans to date and further action needed in the light of experience.

Stage Two

Stage two of the operator workshop took place when the management had crystalised their ideas about the new ways of working they wished to introduce. Stage two was designed to pave the way for these changes. A day was allocated to the programme, and a room away from the shopfloor was booked. The supervisor took the headman role, as he was to be responsible (with support) for the implementation of the new ways of working.

The overall programme was similar to those developed for the other workshops:

1 Informing workshop members about the reasons for the organisation development programme and progress to date.
2 Providing an opportunity for the workshop members to make their feelings known, and for any hostilities to be managed.
3 Identifying problems and developing action plans to overcome the problems.

A great deal of effort was put into developing material for this workshop. In company X it was planned for the initial workshop to be run for operator groups who were seen by management as having the greatest potential for the successful introduction of significant changes in the way work is managed, i.e. job redesign, autonomous work groups, quality circles. However, it is the objective of the organisation development programmes to involve, when the time is right, and in a planned way, all the operator work groups in workshops. Ultimately the objective is to involve all operators in some form of new working practices. All the time and effort in preparing professional material to be used at an operator workshop will, therefore, be worthwhile. In an organisation employing 2,000 plus, it could be used over 100 times and have a major impact, if followed up and supported, on the generation of the desired organisation culture.

Operator workshops are the most difficult to run. The workshop approach requires that the people taking part accept that they should feel involved and that they wish to make a contribution. The participants must exchange views, argue and plan as well as listen passively. The shopfloor operator, partly because of his past experiences at work, partly because of his lack of self-confidence, and partly because of his lack of skill, is less likely to accept a participant's role. He is more likely to be negative and sceptical. Yet in many ways they are the most important workshops. If we cannot get changes in the 'sharp end' that lead to improved effectiveness and commitment, there is little point in starting an organisation development process in the first place.

Outcome

The outcome of a successful operator workshop is a work group willing and able to work with management to change the way they do their jobs. The precise nature of the change will vary from one organisation to another, but would incorporate changes in job design, team working and/or increased involvement in decision making. This workshop will lay the foundation for the introduction of these new working practices.

The process of introducing job redesign, group working or quality circles is not discussed in this book. This omission is not because they are not important, they are essential for the achievement of a committed culture. They are omitted because of lack of space, and because there is a comprehensive literature that describes their practical applications in organisations. This book is about preparing an organisation for these initiatives.

For more information, consult the reading list at the end of the book.

8 Workshops to Facilitate Change

The three workshops described in this chapter are not, strictly speaking, an essential part of an organisation development programme. Each, however, can make a contribution towards the effective implementation of change, but in three very different ways.

1 The organisation audit is concerned with regular long-term reviews during which the work team participates in problem solving and planning activities to overcome obstacles and identify the objectives to be achieved.
2 The building intergroup cooperation workshop removes blockages to change and development by breaking down conflicts between groups.
3 The boss–work team workshop reinforces a management style based on consultation, trust and open communication, and clarifies the expectations the boss and subordinates have of each other.

Organisation audit

Objectives

The organisation audit is a brief and uncomplicated workshop whose objectives are to help a work team plan action to adjust to a changing environment. The need to change is revealed through two things:

1 The work team is having recurrent problems.
2 The work team has identified that tasks they are to perform in the future will be different from the tasks they have been performing in the past.

If no problems can be identified, and the work team is to perform exactly the same task next year as this year then the environment is unchanging and no action will be needed. There are few organisations who find themselves in this situation, so the audit invariably identifies problems to be dealt with, and action to be planned. If the work problems can be overcome, and if the work team is changing its role so that it meets the new challenges and expectations of the future, then it will be systematically going through a process of adjustment which will ensure that it plays its part in ensuring overall organisation effectiveness and flexibility.

The organisation audit is best managed as an annual event. It is an opportunity for a work team to step back from the day-to-day and think about their vision of the future. It is also an opportunity to review if the team's priorities when dealing with the day-to-day problems are the right ones, and if not what should be done about it. At the end of an organisation audit the work team should have a clear idea of what their priorities will be for the next year, and each member should feel commitment to ensuring the team's goals are met.

The organisation audit complements the appraisal system. Where the audit establishes group goals and action to achieve those goals, the annual appraisal establishes the goals that each individual team member must have in order to ensure the success of the work group. The organisation audit should therefore precede the annual appraisal.

In an organisation where the habit of consultation and participation has become part of the culture, an audit can (and should) take place with all work groups: managers, supervisors, operators and specialists. The annual audit should use the 'cascade down' principle. The top mangement team should have the widest vision and the longest time scale, and should therefore make strategic decisions that will impact on their junior colleagues. These top management strategic decisions, and their 'vision' of the future are clearly things that the work teams at lower levels would need to know before they begin their audit. Middle managers would make decisions that impact on supervision. Operators should understand the outcome of the supervisor audit workshop before they embark upon theirs.

The objectives of this workshop can be summarised as follows:

1 To identify any changes between the role the team is currently playing, and that which they will play in the future.
2 To identify the problems that the team are currently having.

3 To identify the action that is needed to make the change from the current role to the future role, and the action needed to solve the current problems.
4 To plan implementation of the action needed.

Programme

An organisation audit takes one day. As usual, a location away from the normal workplace is best. The leader of the work group would act as headman. The audit begins with the headman setting the scene: explaining why the audit is necessary and what he hopes will be achieved. He then makes a presentation to the team. The presentation should inform the team members of the results of the audits of any higher level team, and should also provide for any other information needs that the team might have that must be satisfied before they can embark on the exercise.

The next part of the programme is to develop a vision of the future environment in which the team will operate and of the changes in roles the team must play in order to adjust to that new environment. The most effective way of doing this is by using an approach copied by organisation specialists from ecology, and called an 'open systems modelling', the reader is referred to the suggested reading for more details of how to do open systems modelling. If this approach is considered either too elaborate or too time consuming, a brainstorming session provides an alternative way of developing the vision.

The open system modelling would take the workshop to the lunch break. After lunch two sessions would take place before the headman summarises and concludes the day. The first of these sessions is designed to identify the problems the group feels need to be tackled. A brainstorming approach suits this task well. It would allow the creative identification of the problems and the setting of priorities.

The second afternoon session concerns action planning. In this session two questions are asked:

1 What do we need to do to solve the problems which we identified as having priority?
2 What do we need to do in order to manage the change from the tasks we are performing now to the tasks that we will be performing in the future?

The how, when, who, where and what aspects of these two questions need answering during this action planning session.

Outcome

The outcome of the audit is a blueprint for managing the process of change. A further outcome is the strengthening of the cohesion of the team. The organisation audit is best managed as a workshop, and therefore must follow the workshop rules. The rules require that the headman sets the scene, listens to the discussions and decisions of his team, and ensures that the action plans are carried out during the ensuing year. It is, therefore, an exercise in participation with all the advantages that brings, in the development of the understanding of the participants and their commitment to implement the action plans.

Building intergroup cooperation

Objectives

One of the weaknesses of large, traditional 'role' organisations as described by Handy (see Chapter One) is that the various departments (marketing, manufacturing, quality, engineering and personnel) seem to behave as if they were competing with each other rather than working together to improve the overall effectiveness of the organisation and to provide a cheaper, highest quality, product or a better service. Marketing blame manufacturing for not producing on time, manufacturing feel quality are aloof and unhelpful and that engineering do not appreciate the difficulties of changing the manufacturing process to conform with their latest cost-saving design change. Clearly to be effective an organisation must have high levels of cooperation among the different units. Such cooperation will be much more likely to be achieved after the structural changes proposed in Chapter Four, but even after such a restructured organisation has bedded down, there will frequently be groups of people who have problems working with other groups. Usually the relationship difficulties occur when one group provides a service which the other group consumes. The machine shop manager accuses the machine tool buyers of not being interested in problems with his new machine once it has been formally signed over; the manager of spares marketing feels that components manufacturing do not meet their commitments, the production manager feels that the buyer's latest cost-cutting exercise is leaving him with inferior components.

This workshop is designed to build cooperation between two such groups. In summary the workshop does this by getting each group to see the world through the eyes of the other group, so that they can appreciate the other group's problems, and so that they can appreciate the effect their own behaviour is having in generating difficulties for the other group. Once this empathy has been achieved, the workshop members direct their attention towards planning action which will lead to improvement in cooperation and working relationships.

This workshop is a rather different exercise from the other workshops described in this chapter, in that it involves two groups of people exploring each other's world rather than the growth and development of a single group. It is also unique in that the headman does not take part, his role is delegated. It is however, still very much part of the workshop approach and all the rules laid out in Chapter Five apply equally to this workshop as to any other. This workshop can be critically important in unblocking obstacles to change and in improving working relationships. The blockages have the potential for inhibiting progress of the organisation development programme, because they break down team work between peers, and because they make it more difficult to develop commitment to joint action to work together to achieve organisation change. Given the right preparation and skilled leadership, this workshop is invariably successful in breaking down these blockages. It is also usually quite fun.

The building intergroup cooperation workshop is used when the headman has identified two groups within his organisation with whose level of cooperation he is not satisfied. He will have tried talking to the managers on a one-to-one basis, he will have tried lecturing to the people either singly or in groups, he will have tried the verbal equivalent of knocking their heads together. There will have been occasions when these efforts appeared to bring about improvements only for each group to return after a few days to their slit-trenches to continue sniping at each other. At this stage the headman decides on a workshop approach and selects a workshop leader or catalyst to run it for him. The choice of the leader is critical. His job is to prepare the two groups, gain their commitment to the exercise, and run the workshop. He must be seen as neutral and credible by both parties. He must not be seen as having any personal axe to grind. He must be knowledgable and experienced in running workshops and in the rather different techniques required for this one. The workshop leader may be an outside consultant, but could also be an organisation member, as long as the knowledge, credibility and neutrality criteria are met.

In summary the objectives of this workshop are:

1 To increase the understanding each group has of the other's tasks, responsibilities and problems.
2 To increase the understanding each group has of itself.
3 To increase the understanding each group has of how they themselves are seen by the other group.
4 To identify those issues that are causing problems in relationships between the two groups, and which, if resolved, would lead to a more effective performance by one or both groups.
5 To develop action plans to overcome these identified problems.

Programme

The participants will arrive at the workshop with some apprehension and distrust. The atmosphere will be somewhat brittle. The workshop should be held on neutral ground, ideally away from all the workshop members' normal workplace. The leader begins by reminding the members of the purpose of the day, and outlining the programme. He then moves on to the first session – creative thinking.

The leader makes a short 5–10 minutes presentation emphasising that creative thinking is different from 'normal' thinking and that one of the objectives of the workshop is for each group to see the other in a new light. He will also briefly explain how people can think more creatively (creative thinking is important for most workshops: the reader who wishes to follow up this topic is referred to the reading list at the end of the book). He then invites them to begin their first task – for each group to draw a picture which illustrates how they feel about the other group. The reaction to this suggestion varies: hostility, incredulity, amusement, cynicism. There is something immoral to the puritan within us for grown men and women to spend an hour of the company's time drawing pictures. Somewhat reluctantly even the sceptics eventually agree, and armed with flip-charts and lots of coloured pens, they go to their separate rooms and begin the task. To their surprise it is fun and enlightening. Each group discusses how they see the other group, and how those feelings can be represented in visual form. If there is an artist present, the resulting cartoon can be of a high standard. It will invariably be creative, and the exercise will help all the members of the group crystalise their feelings about both individuals in the other group, and the other group as a whole.

The two groups then come together and each explains their picture to the other group. There will be lots of symbolisms which need explaining but some of the people in the picture will be recognisable. The explanations will be received with a great deal of laughter, and some discomfort, but little offence. Each group will have a much clearer idea of how the others see them.

This exercise communicates effectively and without threat or formality what each group feels about the other. One of the objectives of the workshop is to build within each group a much better understanding of the way the other groups think and feel. It is seen as a 'bit of fun' but the learning is no less valid because of that. This exercise also has the crucial role of beginning to break down the emotional barriers that have been constructed in the past during the period of conflict and mutual distrust.

The second part of the programme is an open systems analysis designed to identify the internal and external influences within each groups' environment. It is used here to clarify the thoughts and concepts each group has about itself and its work and then to communicate those thoughts and concepts to the other group. The open system analysis provides for a systematic communication from each group to the other on how each see their own working environment. After an initial presentation by the workshop leader on the nature of open systems, and on how to construct a model, the two groups go to their separate rooms to complete the task. They then meet together and each group in turn presents their completed model to the other. The non-presenting group is expected to show listening skills; they may ask questions to clarify but it is not permitted to make value judgements or any other comments. The role of one group is to explain their world, the role of the other is to appreciate how this world looks from the presenters' point of view.

The pictures were about communication feelings and emotional reactions, the open system analysis is more about communicating facts and concrete ideas. If either or both groups have developed an open systems model of their own working environment (through for instance, the organisation audit process), this model can be used for this exercise.

The completion of the open systems analysis will take the programme to lunch. Ideally lunch should be a buffet. It is always interesting to see who is talking to whom. It gives the leader some guide as to his success at the half-way stage, in breaking down the barriers.

After lunch both groups do an expectation analysis, which involves each group dealing with what they expect in terms of goods and services from the other group. The precise nature of these questions will depend upon the relationships between the two groups, and the issues that have been revealed in the morning sessions. If one group provides a service to the other the questions would be a variation on:

> The service receiving group:
> What services do I need from you to satisfy my requirements?
> What do I think you believe I need?
>
> The service giving group:
> What services am I going to provide for you based on my concept of services I believe you need?
> What do I think you believe I should provide?

In addition both groups prepare answers to the following:

> What you do that:
> (*a*) annoys us
> (*b*) presents us with difficulties
> (*c*) makes our job more difficult.

When the answers to these questions have been prepared, the two groups come together and exchange presentations.

The objectives of the morning session were to increase each group's understanding of the world from the other's point of view, whilst building an atmosphere that would allow for the confrontation of the issues causing friction between the groups. If the morning has been successful, the expectation analysis will generate the main issues that require confrontation in an atmosphere where the people feel able to accept them, not as an aggressive act of criticism, but as a problem which needs the efforts of both groups to solve. The leader will continue to ensure that listening skills are practised. It is the role of each group to understand what the other group is saying, and therefore it is legitimate to ask for clarification but not to give value judgements.

The final session concerns action planning. Each group now takes the results of the other group's expectation analysis back to their work room. They consider what action they should take to confront the issues that have been causing problems in the past and which, if resolved, would lead to both improved relationships between the groups and a more effective performance by both groups. The groups then again meet together and each informs the other what action they intend to take, and, where no action is to be taken, why not. The leader will again not allow discussion other than for clarification, but he will note down areas where he feels the issues have not been adequately dealt with.

Outcome

If the workshop has gone well both groups will feel that they understand each other better, and feel more positively towards each other. They will believe that things will happen to put right at least some of the problems they had in the past. They will go home feeling that they have had a worthwhile day. But the job of the leader will not be over. The leader still has two crucial roles to play:

1 He must work with each manager to identify how the effectiveness of the action plans is going to be measured, he must review these measurements, and he must set up joint group meetings periodically to assess progress.
2 He must identify those areas (if any) which were not confronted at the workshop and which, if not dealt with, would continue to sour relationships. He must act as an 'honest broker' to see that the issues are recognised and that action is initiated to deal with them.

In order to play these key roles the leader must maintain the perception of himself as neutral, credible, knowledgable, and supportive. These are valuable skills and attributes to have, especially in an organisation struggling to change its management style and philosophy to one which encourages involvement and commitment. The more managers that are trained and practiced in these skills, the more there will be a pool of talent within the organisation able to support and encourage organisation development.

Building boss-team relationships

Objectives

In the management planning workshop held at the beginning of company X's organisation development programme the workshop members began the task of identifying the problems that would have to be overcome if organisation change was to be effectively managed. One of the problems identified was: 'How do we increase our skills and knowledge to be able to manage effectively within the new organisation'. The management group were expressing a concern that their management style would not complement the new philosophy, which seemed to emphasise development of subordinates, delegation of authority and responsibility, trust rather than control, listening rather than instructing, autonomy and generally maximising the potential of all employees. The management group recognised the importance of the organisation development programme, and felt that they would have to change if they were to play their part in both changing the culture and managing within the new culture. At that stage they were not sure how to change, or into what they had to change.

The 'management principles' workshop helped crystalise these concepts. After this workshop they were able to define their learning needs more clearly, and therefore were able to establish a training plan for themselves. Part of this plan would involve training courses which all managers would attend and which would concentrate on building skills and increasing understanding of techniques of man management, and particularly techniques of managing immediate subordinates. A workshop approach to building boss-work team relationships complements this training programme, by providing a forum where a more effective working relationship between boss and subordinate can be developed.

This workshop requires that the subordinates taking part feel that they are able to be open and to confront the boss with the problems he is giving them. If this trusting relationship does not exist, the workshop will not achieve its objectives. Also if the boss is not willing to be open and honest, the workshop will fail. A successful building boss-subordinate relationship workshop is itself a demonstration of the existence of trust based on an open, listening and consultatory style.

The overall objectives are to clarify roles, improve working relationships, build team commitment, and ensure that people are managed in conformity to the management principles. More specifically the objectives of this programme are:

1 To clarify tasks of the boss.
2 To review and negotiate how, when, where and with whom these tasks are carried out.
3 To review, negotiate and clarify the roles of the other group members in supporting the boss in carrying out his tasks.
4 To reinforce an open and consultative management style.

Programme

The boss begins by writing down on a flip-chart what he considers his job to be. He need not prepare carefully, a certain amount of spontaneity helps build an atmosphere that encourages discourse. The other members of the workshop clarify what he is saying by questioning and asking the boss to expand on points. The boss goes into detail when reviewing his tasks, responsibilities and objectives of the hows, wheres, whats and with whoms. He invites his subordinates to identify disagreements and conflicts.

This process is known as an expectation analysis or role analysis. It is best done just after the boss's annual appraisal because he will recently have had his tasks defined, but before the workshop boss appraises his people.

The expectation analysis can generate a great deal of lively discussion. The boss is surprised that his subordinates had so little grasp of what he was trying to achieve. Some bosses even feel guilty about this. Subordinates are often equally surprised; they had the wrong perception of how the boss saw his management role, and had therefore not been reacting to the boss in the most effective way.

The next stage in this workshop is for the boss to take each of his subordinates in turn and to identify what he expects them to do to support his role. Again he seeks to generate discussion and invites from all participants additions, subtractions, clarifications, endorsements and disagreements. If the workshop is being successful, the discussion will be long and lively, and the workshop members will all be enjoying themselves.

Outcome

This workshop can generate a great deal of learning, particularly for the boss. This learning should be translated into action to bring about improvements, so part of the exercise should be to produce an action plan. This is best done by the boss on the following day. He would write down a list of:

1 Things he intends to do differently because of his learning at the workshop.
2 Things that his subordinates are going to do differently because of their learning at the workshop.

This list should be discussed, modified and agreed at a meeting of all participants. It then becomes an action plan, to be reviewed regularly and publically to ensure progress.

The boss-work team workshop is not intended to be a substitute for any of the other planning activities that are involved in boss-subordinate relationships: appraisals, work planning, objective setting, problem solving, individual coaching, identification of training needs. However, it should complement them as the objective of the workshops is the same as the objective of many of these activities: to let people know where they stand and what is expected of them, two-way communication, increased knowledge, increased commitment, improved performance. The workshop is a group activity, designed to build on each member's knowledge and abilities and to develop common understanding and so develop a group of people able and willing to work together, and all pulling in the same direction, to achieve the team's goals.

9 Union Workshop

This chapter is about gaining the cooperation of the union in an organisation development programme. The proposals presented are based on the assumption that although clearly there will always be some conflict of interests between management and unions, both benefit from the success and growth of the organisation as a whole. There will, therefore, be many areas where both management and union will benefit from cooperation. In particular both will benefit from cooperating to develop and implement plans to increase organisation effectiveness. The assumption is also made that management get from unions the behaviour they expect. If management assume in their dealings with the unions that there is a conflict of interest, then the employee relations atmosphere will be conflictory. If management assumes there are wide areas of potential agreement, they will behave towards the union in a way that generates a cooperative attitude. This chapter is about how to bring about and maintain union cooperation through developing an atmosphere of trust and a mutual commitment to long-term objectives of benefit to all.

There are two basic themes:

1. Management must understand the thinking, concerns, problems and needs of union representatives if they are to provide an atmosphere where the union is comfortable in taking a co-operative stance.
2. Management and union must meet together in an atmosphere where information is freely given, and where people have the opportunity to work through their concerns, and to listen to

each other's views. In such an atmosphere the identification of problems is seen as an opportunity for organisation improvements rather than laying blame, and genuine search is made for action that will be to the long-term advantages of the organisation and all its members. It must be the management who take the initiative in generating this atmosphere.

Union relations: conflict or cooperation

Most headmen in commercial, industrial and governmental organisations who are trying to introduce change will find themselves spending a considerable amount of time dealing with their trade unions. In many of these organisations the majority of the management will believe that the trade union is the biggest single inhibitor to change within the system. In some of these organisations this management view may well appear correct. Managers will point to a long history of union intransigence when they have been asked to cooperate in introducing change. These managers, and the unions with whom they interact, will have a conflicting model of industrial relations. Such a model sees organisation change as one part of the process of capital seeking to exploit labour more effectively; thus the role of the union must be to resist that change.

In this chapter the assumption is made that union-management relations in organisations are not usually characterised by conflict, and that where the industrial relations climate is hostile, it need not be. The union's hostility towards change is a product of the way they have been treated in the past. Where the union has not been kept informed and has not been consulted on matters that they feel are important to their members they will feel that management will have inhibited them in their (to them) legitimate role of protecting their members' interests. They will feel powerless to influence events, yet pressured from two directions: management and their own membership. In such situations the union will resist change and try to extract the maximum short-term advantage, because this course of action will make them least vulnerable to censure from their own members. If this assumption is correct we can do something about union behaviour by changing the way management behave.

The theme, as with other parts of this book, is that organisations can behave in a way that builds understanding and trust; in this case trust between management and trade unions. As this understanding and trust develops, so will greater commitment to organisation goals and greater flexibility and therefore, the capacity to adjust to a changing environment. These changes can only take place if the right policies are consistently followed by management over many years. These policies are not complex or novel. They involve improving the quality and quantity of information provided to unions, consulting with unions on management 'visions' and action plans, and asking for active participation and involvement in some of these plans. If these things happen, then over time, and with many hiccups, the cooperation and commitment will come that will transform the union to facilitator of change, rather than what they often appear; a conservative bureaucracy that resists change proposed by far-sighted managers.

This chapter covers a topic that will be treated by many managers in Western commercial and industrial organisations with the greatest degree of scepticism. The idea that their organisation's union could become trusting, flexible and committed to overall organisation effectiveness is not a reality they can envisage. Yet there are organisations in all (without exception) sections of our commercial and industrial world where union-management relations are effective for all concerned. These organisations are usually new, often foreign owned (including Japanese) and invariably successful. It is the variations in quality of employee relations between organisations that demonstrates the scope for improvement in so many.

No assumption is made that there is not some inevitable conflict between unions and decision makers in organisations. Clearly there will be conflicts over rewards and benefits, over technological changes that make jobs redundant, over the existence of restricted practices. There will always be short and medium term conflicts which result in confrontation and can be resolved only through the use of power, and over the negotiating table. In dealing with trade unions management would be acting suicidally if they always adopted a 'participatory' stance. Nor is it being argued that organisation change can only be brought about through consultation and participation. Many changes can be brought about quickly and efficiently using the power that many managements have to impose their decisions on the workforce. Change should be brought about in this way if speed is essential. If management has the power to force change, the union might not like it, but there is little they can do about it. However, such an authoritarian approach would only be effective in the short term.

The regular use of 'power' to impose decisions has long-term effects. It reinforces the conflictual nature of management-union relations, and makes management vulnerable to changes in the balance of power. The use of authoritarian tactics will inhibit the growth of an atmosphere in an organisation where all the members are committed to that organisations' long-term success, for the benefit of all. The more the members are informed and involved, the greater will be the chance of developing this atmosphere. The approach that management takes to the union can break down the 'natural' conflicts, and encourage the search for 'natural' alliances. If union representatives can be helped to understand the overall business situation, and if they are given the opportunity to work through long-term strategic plans (such as an organisation development programme), they can learn to appreciate that management planning is designed to ensure the long-term success of the organisation, which implies the long-term satisfaction of the needs of the union and its members. They may even be able to make a contribution to that planning. Approaching the union in this way may lead to very different behaviour from that which we usually find in union-management contacts.

The union representative: does he bleed?

We have asserted in this chapter that we need an effective long-term working relationship with any union if we are to achieve high levels of commitment and the capacity on the part of the union to think strategically. In order to achieve this union-management relationship, management must involve the unions and must keep them informed, and they also must avoid the use of power to impose change, even though its use may be efficient in the short term.

In this section the focus is on the trade unionist: what makes him tick and what does he want (for himself and for his union) from effective cooperation to bring about change. Only by understanding the world from the union's perspective can we understand the union's needs, and can we search for ways of meeting those needs so that we maximise the chance of union cooperation in the process of implementing change. If management understand the way unionists think and feel, they will be more able to identify 'win-win' situations. They will also be more able to understand the conflict implicit in 'win-lose' situations, and therefore be able to handle confrontations more effectively.

This section attempts to describe a 'typical' union representative working within a 'typical' union. Yet all unions vary and certainly each is made up of a collection of different individuals. This description is inevitably something of a caricature, but hopefully a pattern is described that makes sense to people within unions, or people who interact with unionists in their organisations. If it does not make sense then the reader will reject it (and so he should) and he will also reject the recommendations which are based on this perspective.

The average trade union representative:

1 Feels that he never has all the facts. Most of his information comes from the personnel manager, who does not give away

information that could be used against management in a negotiating situation. Sometimes a director comes to talk to the union representatives, but when that happens there is usually something wrong and he often feels that he is not being communicated with, he is being preached at. If his organisation has a regular 'briefing notes' communicating system, then he is less likely to feel deprived of information. If his organisation has some form of union-management joint consultation process which has genuine top management support, he may even feel that management make a genuine attempt to communicate. But he has learned from experience that although they may never tell him lies, they frequently do not tell him the whole truth. He always feels they know more than he does, and that they have a crucial advantage in any negotiation.

2 Is determined not to be outdone in an argument by management. They may have been to university but that does not make them better people. Just because they can use long words it does not mean that they have a better argument. If he is feeling baffled he will become aggressive, play for time (use the procedures), dig in his heels, become obstinate. But management are not going to get the better of him!

3 Sees himself and his colleagues as the people who do the most to ensure a smoothly-running organisation. They are the people who handle the endless problems that shopfloor people have due to the unthinking and selfish behaviour and attitudes of supervision and management. They act as intermediaries and catalysts to get things put straight before they grow into major conflicts.

4 Gets his status from being seen as being able to handle management, and being seen as a major influence with whom management must come to terms. The annual negotiation may be a ritual whose outcome is entirely predictable, but it is a necessary ritual to reinforce the role of the trade unionist and legitimise that role in the eyes of his members. If management try to minimise his role, he will react by creating the crisis that requires his cooperation to solve. People who are good at solving crises, benefit from creating them. Providing him with information that he can pass on enhances his status. Giving it him before the supervisor enhances it even more (but this is not recommended if a good relationship with the supervisor is to be maintained).

5 Gets his satisfaction from helping his members with their problems, and feels a great deal of pressure from below to represent their short-term interests. If he is seen in conference with

management, especially if he is known to have confidential information, he will come under suspicion for putting the company or his own interests before his members'. It is difficult for him to act as a statesman, easy for him to act as a trouble-maker.

6 Is loyal to his union, his members and his organisation, and not necessarily in that order. He wants to be proud of his organisation and his role within it: he wants it to succeed and to feel that he has made a contribution to that success.

7 Feels pressured from all sides because his union membership, his union leadership, and the organisation's management, each want different things from him and each has different expectations.

8 Feels that the odds are always against him. Ultimately management have the power to impose and the union is only really able to be a nuisance. When it comes to the crunch, he cannot rely on the support of his fickle membership, whilst management have all the resources of the organisation behind them.

The trade union representative's behaviour reflects the world as he sees it. He feels at a disadvantage because of his lack of training and education, and because he is not kept fully informed. He reacts to these feelings of inadequacy with aggression and when pressured with belligerence and obstinacy. He feels pressured from all sides. He reacts to these pressures by attempting to play political games (usually not very successfully) and by behaving inconsistently as he responds to different outside pressures. He feels he is doing an important (though difficult) job and wants to make a contribution. He will be willing, even anxious to make a positive contribution to the process of increasing organisational effectiveness if he can be made to feel confident and adequate to the job, if trust has been developed, if he believes that what he is doing will be for the benefit of his union and its members, and if he can be helped to manage the role-conflict that will inevitably come from working closely with management.

The next section is concerned with how company X moved towards a more fruitful, long-term relationship with trade union representatives.

The management–union workshop

Objectives

A workshop for union representatives must be designed differently from other workshops because of three factors:

1 Union representatives have problems, expectations and values that are different from those of any other group in an organisation. These differences are discussed in the previous section and should be taken into consideration when designing a workshop. It could be argued that union representatives have to be dealt with more carefully.
2 A union is itself an organisation with its own rules and hierarchy. The workshop design must recognise this. This can best be done by consulting with the union on the design, preparation and running of the workshop, by ensuring the programme is acceptable to the union, and by inviting the senior union representative to run the introductory and concluding sessions jointly with the most senior manager. The union workshop has two headmen; one from the union and one from management.
3 This workshop is more properly called a joint management-union workshop. Although there will be part of the programme where management is presenting information to the union the more important parts are best seen as an exchange of views between two groups. A union workshop must, therefore, have a significant management presence.

The management at company X took these factors into consideration when planning their workshop with the union.

At their planning workshop, and at the management principles workshop, company X management came to the conclusion that a new relationship with the union was needed. They developed a clear idea of what this relationship would be like, and what they had to do to achieve it. They resolved to invite the union to join them for a workshop. Because they believed in a 'cascade down' approach to organisation development, the timing of this workshop was critical. The decision was taken to have this workshop after the programme of supervisor workshops had been completed, but before any operator workshops. The 'cascade down' approach assumes that changes in the behaviour and attitude of management and supervision must take place before changes in the behaviour and attitude of the union can be expected. The organisation development programme had been in existence in company X for well over a year before a union-management workshop took place.

The overall objectives of the union-management workshop are the same as the objectives of all the other workshops: to develop a set of beliefs and attitudes which lead workshop members to feel committed to the long-term success of the organisation. There should be no long-term conflicts of interest here; both union representatives and union members are members of the organisation and benefit from its long-term viability. The short-term conflicts between management and unions that will inevitably arise from time to time, will be much easier to resolve if both groups have a common vision of where the organisation is going and how they are going to get there.

More specifically the objectives of the workshop run for the management and unions in company X were as follows:

1 To inform union representative of:
   (*a*) The reasons for the organisation development programme;
   (*b*) The principles and philosophies that are guiding the organisation development programme;
   (*c*) The progress to date.
2 To consult with and exchange views with the union on the organisation development programme.
3 To review ways in which the union should be consulted, or otherwise involved in implementing the organisation development programme.
4 To introduce to the union some of the concepts of human resource management used by management to develop the management principles.

Programme

In company X, the union had been aware that the organisation development programme existed but had little clear idea of what it was all about. They were feeling that, as usual, managers were planning things that would have a major impact on their members, without any consultation. They had asked the personnel manager what it was all about, but he had been vague and told them that they would be told all about it when the time was right. It came as something of a relief to the union representatives when they were invited to discussions on the organisation development programme. They were cooperative in discussions about the design of the workshop and generally wanted it to be as similar as possible to the supervisory workshops.

The workshop was held in a local hotel. As the workshop members gathered for an early cup of coffee the atmosphere was a little tense and some of the representatives appeared truculent, possibly to cover up their feelings of nervousness and apprehension. Two representatives were late (unheard of at the supervisory workshop) but most were very early.

The management headman opened the proceedings. He explained why the management had invited the union to the workshop, what he hoped would be the outcome, and he outlined the programme. The union headman then made his introductory remarks. He welcomed the workshop and looked forward to an exchange of views and to being consulted on the organisation development programme. He also remarked that the workshop would only be valuable if the discussions were open and honest. He felt that it put a responsibility on both union and management to use the information positively to aid the growth of understanding. If union comments were to be used against them in future bargaining positions, then the workshop would do more harm than good. The management headman endorsed the union headman's comments (he had had a long session with the personnel manager discussing management concerns on the same issue).

The management headman then made a presentation on why the organisation development programme was felt to be necessary. He emphasised the worldwide competitive situation, and the performance levels of Japanese manufacturing organisations. He used good quality visual aids and attempted to be factual and avoid judgement. He answered questions (there were only a few), but at this stage did not encourage discussion. The union representatives were attentive and appeared interested. The tape of the managing director explaining the corporate management philosophy was then played. Comments were invited, few were made. The management headman then told the workshop about how the management principles had been developed, briefly went through their content and gave each union representative a copy.

The union representatives were then invited to work in groups of 5 to 7, discussing what they had heard so far, and in particular what concerns they had with the philosophy. They were quite willing to do this (there had been some speculation that they would not be), and went to their separate rooms armed with cups of coffee. In workshop design this first discussion session is expected to reveal and manage any frustration and hostile feelings. It was expected, therefore, that the feedback session would be emotionally charged, with the union showing feelings of hostility towards the management. But it did not turn out that way. Each union group made presentations with similar content. They endorsed (with some reservations) the management philosophy, and said that it was about time that the management made these changes. They then produced a long list of concerns about the way the programme would be implemented. This list is provided in Appendix Six, but the three main concerns were these:

1 *Security*. Change means that some jobs will disappear, whilst others will require new skills. People will find difficulty in cooperating with new ways of doing things if they feel they may be working themselves out of a job. The company therefore must take the necessary steps to reassure people about their long-term security.

2 *Speed of change*. Management will try to implement change faster than the people can come to terms with it.
3 *Training*. Management will not support changes by training programmes to give the union members the different skills and knowledge they require.

The management headman chaired the feedback sessions. All the managers had been well briefed on what was expected of them – to practice their listening skills. They asked for clarification, appeared (and were) interested in what the representatives had to say, they avoided value judgements and pushing forward their own views. The quality of the presentations surprised the managers, and the union presenters became more confident as it became clear that managers were interested, were listening and were not trying to put them down. At the end of the session the apprehension had largely disappeared. Both headmen were feeling 'so far, so good'.

Over a buffet lunch the managers speculated over why the session had been so matter-of-fact: very different from their own first workshop, and the workshops that had been run for specialists and supervision. They decided that the organisational development programme was not as threatening to the union as it was to the other groups, at least at this stage. Managers, supervisors and specialists knew the change programme meant new problems, new responsibilities, the possibility of not being able to cope or loosing status. The union did not see themselves as having these problems, hence the lack of hostility and frustration, and the anti-climax.

The afternoon sessions consisted of two presentations. The first was on developments to date in the organisation development programme. The union group showed great interest, particularly in the views expressed and problems identified in the other workshops. There was a great deal of discussion and many questions. The session ran over its allotted time. The second presentation was on Flagtown (the plant run on principles based on the corporate management philosophy). Again there was a great deal of discussion and many questions. The union began to think through the implications of what was being said for their own positions, particularly the absence of any demarcations at Flagtown. The management headman nearly fell off his chair when he heard the union headman make the comment that the current levels of demarcations would have to go, if levels of efficiency were to improve and the organisation was to become more effective. The union representatives endorsed this. They also wanted a more effective competitive organisation, and believed this could not be achieved if the union operated restricted practices. As the afternoon continued the managers joined in more. There was some friendly banter, but the managers were careful to maintain their listening roles. The session went one-and-a-half hours over the allotted time. The union did not ask for overtime payment, they were having a good time!

The workshop was residential. After dinner, a great deal of drink was consumed, and the union representatives expected this to be free! The atmosphere was convivial, but for the most part union representatives talked to union representatives, managers to managers.

The opening session on day two, consisted of a guest speaker talking about his experiences in introducing job redesign. The presentation was well received, questions and discussions were relevant. The atmosphere was not, however, as lively as it had been the afternoon before. After coffee both management and union formed small discussion groups. The topic was to think through what each group felt that:

1 It should do about the organisation development programme.
2 What the other group should do about the organisation development programme.

Just over an hour was needed for the small group discussions. There was enough time for the management group to present their thoughts before lunch. The union groups made their presentations after lunch. A summary of these presentations is to be found in Appendix Six. Again discussions were lively and open and again the managers were impressed with the quality of the union presentations. It was clear that the union representatives had taken the opportunity to think through the issues. They wanted to support the programme, but they had also made themselves aware of the difficulties, and were sceptical about management's willingness and capacity to carry it through.

Again the session ran over time, and people were now feeling drained and tired. It was agreed to cancel a planned session on job enrichment and go straight on to the winding-up session.

The management headman said that he was very pleased with both the level and content of the discussions and that he had learned a lot from them. He did not want to commit himself or his management colleagues to any firm action at this point, but consideration would be given to what follow-up action was appropriate. He would make proposals to the union within a month and he anticipated that these proposals would include further meetings to discuss matters of mutual interest concerning the organisation development programme. He then went through the main learning points for him and thanked the union for their attendance.

The union headman said that he thought that the workshop represented a major step forward in management's relations with the union. He hoped that management would maintain this policy of consultation and communication and he looked forward to receiving the management headman's proposals and to further discussions on the organisation development programme. He thanked the management for their hospitality.

Outcome

Union workshops can be very successful. Management teams are frequently astonished at the positive and honest atmosphere created, if only because their level of expectation was so low. If the follow-up is effectively managed, they can be a firm foundation on which to build management-union relations that support change, flexibility and efficiency for the benefit of all the organisation members.

Two of the workshop rules are particularly important in a union workshop. Firstly, because the union feel that management do not communicate with them or listen to them, management listening skills are even more important than in the other workshops. Secondly, the management team should not try to achieve too much. If attempts are made to get the union to commit themselves at an action planning session, the union will feel they are being pressurised. The workshop should be considered a success if, after the event, the union representatives feel that they:

1 Have a better understanding of what is going on.
2 Have thought through the implications of what is being said.
3 Have had their say and been listened to.
4 Feel more comfortable about their relationships with management.

If these things are achieved, a foundation will have been laid for action in the future. This foundation will have been laid through two days of open discussion of the right topics, in the right place, with the right people and in a positive atmosphere. There must now be systematic, planned action to build on this foundation.

Action following the workshop

Although they will react negatively to being pressurised into commitments to action before they fully understand what is going on, the union will expect some follow-up activity. Expectations will have been raised that something will happen. The more the union feel that management have listened to them, the more they will expect management to do something about what they have heard. If management are not prepared to take action about the problems and concerns identified at the workshop, they should not have initiated the process in the first place. The least that should emerge from the workshop is a commitment on the part of everyone present, to meet regularly to discuss the change programme, and a commitment by management to respond to what they have heard at the workshop.

If the workshop has been a success both management and union will welcome a continuation of the process. Who should attend, how frequently the meetings should occur, and what should be discussed can be agreed after the workshop. Usually the initial meetings are convened monthly. In company X it was decided that the negotiating committee should meet with the personnel manager and line managers.

The agenda at the first follow-up meeting was a reinforcement of what happened at the workshop. The management group prepared a summary of the main issues discussed, and any conclusions or commitments, however tentative, that were reached. This summary was discussed, modified as appropriate, and agreed. The management also stated what action they intended to take as a result of the workshop, and when they intended to take it. No commitment to action was looked for from the union at this stage, but as time went on the union became more and more willing to cooperate in the operator workshop programme, and in the introduction, under sheltered agreements, of experiments into new ways of working for their members.

Union involvement in organisation development programmes

The management-union workshop will have laid down the foundations for effective union cooperation in the organisation development programme. However, there are a number of key points that all management using the workshop approach should keep in mind when interacting with the union in order to gain their commitment to, and cooperation with, long-term organisation change. These rules will apply to most situations, but the relevance of each will vary from one situation to another.

1 The union will continuously be looking for a diminution in management commitment. If management commit themselves to action; it must happen. If management are not prepared to take action, they should explain why.
2 At least in the early stages the union should not be expected to join with management in developing detailed plans for organisation changes. They will not know enough about the technical aspects of change, and particularly about job redesign and of autonomous workings to make a meaningful contribution, and they will delay matters with nit-picking and red herrings. Leave the planning to the experts, consult with the union at a stage when you are prepared to modify any plans but where manage-

ment believe them to be workable. If joint union-management working parties are thought necessary, they should be in areas of low technical content, and even then an 'expert' should be assigned to the working party as adviser and scribe.

3 In working closely with management, the union is potentially in a role conflict situation. They have to meet the conflicting expectations of the union hierarchy, of management and of their members. They may need help in handling this conflict.

4 Unions are often dreadful in managing their own affairs and in making effective decisions. Anything management can do to help the union become more effective will be to the long-term benefit of the organisation.

5 The union's appetite for information will grow the more it is fed. Management must understand at the outset that this approach requires time, effort, and commitment to providing information, some of which at least initially will be used against them.

6 The organisation change meeting should not be allowed to become a negotiating forum. Negotiations are about resolving short and medium term conflicts, what the organisation development meeting is about is working together to find long-term solutions to long-term problems. If the organisation change meeting identifies items that need to be negotiated, those items should be referred to the usual negotiating procedures.

7 The union will demand training. As far as it makes sense, these demands should be met.

8 The union will be looking for safeguards for their members. The union will not negotiate any of their members out of a job unless they are convinced that some must be sacrificed for the benefit of the majority. If the interests of any union members are harmed by the change process, the union will always attempt to negotiate some form of compensation. They will try to gain acceptance by management of a set of ground rules to protect their members from the effects of change, usually by establishing some form of new technology agreement. Such an agreement is usually necessary to ensure union cooperation, and management should negotiate with the union in these areas. The organisation change meeting is not the right forum.

9 Management will have made a conscious decision that the benefits of using a consultative approach with the union outweighs the costs. The business environment may change and make a consultation process no longer appropriate. In a redundancy situation management must revert to an authoritarian

stance; they must tell the union that jobs will be lost. The union must then take its traditional role – to oppose. A redundancy situation involving employees at all levels is in many ways an ideal situation to impose major changes. Taking advantage of such a situation may be to the short-term advantage of the organisation. It will however, make it doubly difficult to build cooperation, trust and commitment in the future. The organisation will be seen as one that looks for cooperation when it wants something but puts the boot in when times become difficult. The long-term effects of reverting to 'power' management should be considered by a far-sighted management. Just as a pendulum swings from one side to the other, so does the balance of power in an organisation. If the balance favours management, they will be able to impose change on the unions. But such imposition is likely to result in an unstable situation with the union fighting to redress the balance as the pendulum swings back across. It may sometimes be appropriate to forego short-term advantages, in order to build the right atmosphere within the organisation. The Japanese do! In order to facilitate union cooperation in organisation change, however, the best thing management can do is to ensure a steady employment situation.

Summary and conclusions

Company X was lucky in that they only had one union to deal with. Many organisations will have a number, both white and blue collar. Some of these unions will have hostile relationships with some of the others. Some of the unions will have a head office policy which precludes them from cooperating with organisation development programmes and the introduction of new working methods on the shopfloor. Taking a workshop approach with the unions is often, therefore, much more difficult and complex than has been suggested in this chapter. Not all managers (or unionists) will see the approach recommended in this chapter as practical or workable. Perhaps in their organisation it is not. Certainly unless the rules for running workshops are carefully followed, the management-union workshops can go badly wrong. But it can and does work given determination, persistence, time and effort.

The values put forward in this chapter can be summarised as follows:

1 Unions can and will cooperate in working towards improved organisation effectiveness if they are allowed to.

2 In order to bring about the necessary atmosphere of co-operation and trust management must appreciate the needs of their union representatives, and manage in the way that allows them to be met. These needs are essentially:
   (*a*) To be kept informed;
   (*b*) To feel adequate and confident;
   (*c*) To have a position of status and influence;
   (*d*) To make a contribution;
   (*e*) To handle the different expectations of their members, their union hierarchy and management.

3 In order to meet these needs management must:
   (*a*) Keep the union informed;
   (*b*) Listen to what they have to say and wherever possible act on their suggestions; accept their definitions of the problems to be overcome;
   (*c*) Consult with them on major changes being planned in the way work is organised; where appropriate participate with them in experimental changes under sheltered agreement.

4 Working with unions in this way will have many disadvantages for management:
   (*a*) It is time-consuming;
   (*b*) They will be giving away information, some of which will be used against them later;
   (*c*) They must put resources into handling problems that the union perceive, rather than dealing with priorities that they might consider central;
   (*d*) They will be frustrated by the lack of knowledge and insight on the part of some union representatives;
   (*e*) The union will frequently let management down and fail to meet their commitments.

A manager involved in this long process of relationship building will probably continually ask, 'Is it worth the effort?' The only real answer to that question is: 'What choice is there?' Only through the active cooperation of all its members can we bring about the fully flexible organisation, an organisation that is able to perceive the action that is needed to meet the new threats and opportunities in the business environment, and take that action rapidly. In the long term we must manage our organisation so that this cooperation is maximised. The committed culture cannot be achieved if management-union relations are based on assumptions of conflict and characterised by feelings of mistrust. The Japanese have demonstrated that it can be done. Their UK operations have been able to maintain effective employee relations whilst introducing new technologies.

There is also another reason, one that is about union power. The union will always have a capacity to inhibit progress, sometimes even to sabotage major investment programmes. The need to work with the union is partly a reflection on the need to come to terms with the union's power which, although invariably limited, can potentially be used to inhibit progress.

10 Team Structures

At their principles workshop the company X management decided that they wanted to manage through teams. The guidelines they developed are presented in full in Appendix Two. In summary the main decisions made at the workshop were:

1 Decision making should be vested in the work group.
2 The work group should be autonomous.
3 Specialists tasks should be integrated into the production process to increase team spirit.
4 Supervision should be trained to enable them to play a different role as team leaders in the new organisation.

The managers only discussed the general principles of organising through work teams. They wished to leave the detailed interpretation of these principles to the people responsible for managing in the new way and managing the change process. This ensured that the detailed plans that developed reflected the specific problems and opportunities in each area, and that the people involved felt committed to the plans they had themselves developed. In this chapter the reasons for basing organisations on interlocking work teams is discussed.

The second section of this chapter, describes how an organisation based on a series of interlocking work teams – production teams, support teams and management teams, would look. The benefits of the development of team working is also described.

The third section deals with the problems that are generated when an organisation disbands its functional departments and moves to the organisation of work through teams. The solution to the problems proposed in this section is a matrix approach to organisation structuring. The matrix approach is also relevant to the problems generated by moving to 'business structures' (described in Chapter Four).

The fourth section is not strictly about introducing new structures and designs, but about what these new structures would be like to work in. In particular this section compares the role of the supervisor in traditional company X, and the role of the supervisor in new, developed company X and suggests that the supervisor will be doing less day-to-day problem solving, and be less involved in routine paperwork. He will be more concerned with people development, planning, training, counselling and supporting his operators.

Building manufacturing teams

In the classical organisation structure the supervisor will refer any problems which he cannot manage to the appropriate specialist department. The specialist department will allocate someone to deal with it. If a machine tool is broken down, they will send for an engineer. If the supervisor is having problems with his raw materials, he will refer it to a supply liaison specialist from purchasing. As soon as he refers the problem to someone else he can relax. If he fails to make his targets, it is not his fault. He was not given the service by the functional department. The classic structures breed the 'us *v* them' syndrome. The team concept attempts to break this syndrome down.

Under the manufacturing team concept the starting point for organisation design is the operator. He is the person who actually makes and assembles and pieces, or provides the service to the customer. Without him the organisation achieves nothing. It can be argued, therefore, that he is the most important person in the organisation, and the other members should be organised in a way that ensures that he is given the best possible support. He gets support through being provided with services when he has a problem with which he cannot cope. These services are organised by his supervisor and management, who ultimately therefore, only exist to help the operator do an effective job.

The 'team' concept ensures that the operator is the centre of attention, and at the same time breaks down the 'us *v* them' syndrome. The detailed design of a manufacturing team will vary from organisation to organisation and depends upon the needs and problems that are to be managed. Following the restructuring of company X into businesses, the organisation restructuring concentrated on developing manufacturing teams. The structure of the teams is illustrated in Figure 10.1.

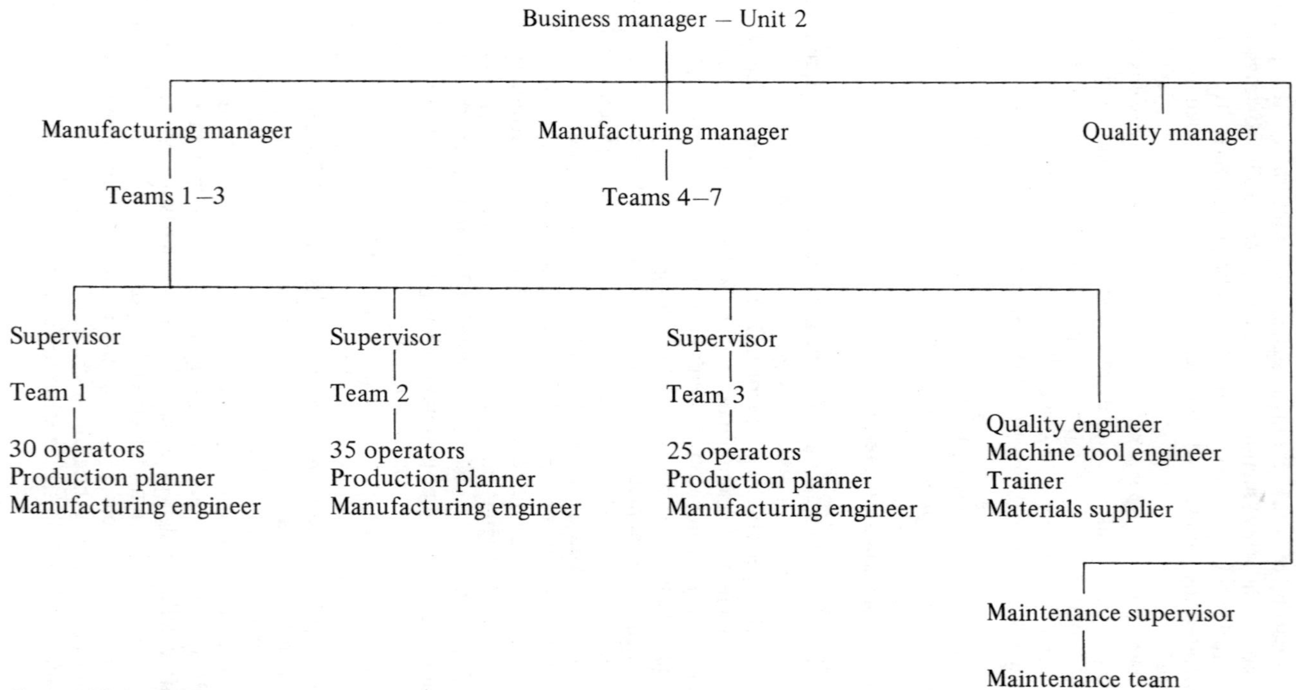

Figure 10.1 Team structure

Two manufacturing managers, a maintenance supervisor, and a quality manager report to the Unit 2 business manager. Each manufacturing manager is responsible for operator teams with their supervisors. He also has reporting to him a number of specialists who provide support to him and to each of his teams as and when they require it. Two specialists do not report directly to him. They work within each team and report to the supervisor: one to support him in planning his production schedules, the other to deal with machining problems. Because the maintenance function provides a service to both the manufacturing managers, they report directly to the business manager.

This structure is designed to maximise the cooperation between people with different skills, and ensure that there is a commitment to providing the best possible service to the operator actually producing the goods or services for the customer.

The main principles illustrated in Figure 10.1 are:

1 The organisation is based on a series of interacting teams:
   (*a*) Supervisors with operators and support specialists;
   (*b*) Manufacturing manager with his supervisors and specialist support staff;
   (*c*) Maintenance supervisor with his maintenance team.
   Each team operates under the rules of autonomous working.
2 The specialists who provide support to the manufacturing teams act as consultants, to be called in by the teams as, and when, they are needed. If they are seen as not performing a good service, they will not be called in; the team will find alternative solutions. The decision is made by the people responsible for getting the job done, not by a functional department manager, who is too often motivated to look after his people, instead of supporting the manufacturing process.
3 The specialist feels part of the manufacturing team, rather than part of a functional department. His feelings of achievement depend upon the success of the manufacturing teams he supports, not on the standing and status of a functional department.
4 The number and location of the specialists are organised according to what makes sense at the time. Figure 10.1 sees the need for a trainer to provide a service to each manufacturing manager: one trainer to three or four teams gives the individual trainer a manageable work load, and the team an effective service. If the need for training increased, then it might be appropriate to have a trainer in each team. If the need for training decreased, one trainer between both manufacturing managers might make sense. This structure together with the

people who man it are flexible.

5 The team concept must be complemented by changes in the role and function of the functional manager. (Each business manager has a responsibility for one functional area; because Figure 10.1 shows the organisation structure for Unit 2, the functional manager is responsible for quality: see pages 50–4 in Chapter Four.) Those changes are discussed in the next section, where it is pointed out that the movement from organisation in specialist departments to organisation in support teams brings problems, and where the methods of overcoming these problems are discussed.

This structure incorporates many of the principles of autonomous group working, and anyone attempting to adopt a structure of this sort should make himself thoroughly familiar with these principles. In this section it is intended to give a flavour of how a manufacturing organisation based on team principles might look, to list the main principles involved, and to persuade the reader that team working brings many significant advantages. Work teams are complex, and difficult to manage, but can result in high levels of individual performance and the efficient integration of the many skills that go to make up the modern organisation. It is difficult to imagine an organisation that achieves high levels of commitment from all its employees without adopting principles of autonomous team working.

Incorporating matrix principles

Organising on the basis of team working implies the break up of functional departments, which is recommended, not only to facilitate the development of work teams, but also to allow for the introduction of 'business structures'. This section deals with the disadvantages of disbanding functional departments but suggests that they can be managed if a matrix approach is adopted.

The dismantling of a functional organisational structure brings with it the following problems that must be overcome:

1 The specialist now works for managers who have little technical knowledge or skills in the specialised areas he offers the organisation. The new boss will be less able to understand his problems, less able to give technical support, and less able to train and coach him.

2 The new structures require that the functional specialist provides a wider range of skills. He becomes less of a specialist and more of a generalist: effectively he is being deskilled.

3 The break-up of a specialist department means that there will no longer be a centre of expertise on which the senior management can rely for policy development and technical advice.
4 The clear promotion structure that would normally exist in a functional department is removed. In our new organisation, with its emphasis on reduced hierarchy and the management of problems of integration through team interaction rather than management decision, there are no clearly marked promotion routes for specialists.

In order to overcome these problems the organisation should adopt a matrix structure. Under such a structure, the specialist would have two bosses: a line manager and a functional manager. The line manager (in Figure 10.1 the manufacturing manager is the line manager) would be responsible for the performance of all the people with direct reporting relationship to him: supervisors and specialists. The specialist would also have a 'dotted line relationship with his functional manager who in company X could well be working in a different 'business'. The functional manager (e.g. the quality manager) would have 'dotted line' responsibility for all the specialists in his functional area in the organisation.

The day-to-day responsibilities of the functional manager for his dotted line subordinate would be to:

1 Provide a specialist technical back-up service when they need help, support or advice.
2 Provide opportunities for specialists to meet regularly with their technical colleagues in order to share experiences and learn from each other in an atmosphere of mutual problem solving.
3 Ensure that the specialist operates within company policies and procedures.
4 Advise on 'pay and ration' issues and ensure equity of treatment for his subordinates in different businesses.
5 Work with the line manager to develop a training plan and be responsible for implementing the plan.

In addition to these responsibilities for individuals, the functional manager would be responsible for manpower planning and succession planning within his functional area. He would therefore be planning the careers of all the specialists working in the different businesses.

The implication of these tasks and responsibilities is that organisations should still maintain small but expert functional departments. In company X, each senior manager had a responsibility for a function. Figure 10.1 shows that this responsibility in the case of the business manager for Unit 2, is for quality. The business manager has a quality manager (a middle manager position) reporting to him. This quality manager would not be responsible for the day-to-day management of the majority of the people in that specialist function. Those people would be dispersed throughout the organisation in the manufacturing teams. The quality manager would, however, have a small team reporting to him who would carry out other responsibilities.

The role of the functional manager does not become less important when, under a matrix structure, he ceases to directly manage lots of people, but it does become different. The functional manager's new role would be to:

1 Recommend to the business manager policies and procedures to guide the management of the function within the total organisation.
2 Audit to ensure that the policies and procedures are being followed and standards maintained.
3 Provide expert advice and assistance to the specialists working in the manufacturing teams.
4 Provide a training service to ensure that all the specialists within his function develop their skills and knowledge.
5 Accept responsibility for ensuring the future supply of specialists with the right skills and in the right numbers by managing policies for recruitment, career development, succession planning and manpower planning.

These are most important tasks. If the specialists are not developed and supported and if standards of performance are not kept high, the long-term consequences for the organisation will be considerable. The functional manager would normally have a small team of experts to assist him. Their jobs would be to act as consultants, auditors and trainers.

The functional manager does not deal with the day-to-day; that is the responsibility of the line manager. It is also the line manager's job to manage the specialist in a way that makes him feel that he is an integral and essential part of the manager's team and only secondary, one of a number of specialists with similar interests.

The small functional departments with these responsibilities will manage the problems that are caused by the development of the team concept and which are listed at the beginning of this section. Such a matrix structure has the potential to optimise the talents of people, build commitment, maximise communications, preserve flexibility and creativity and enrich the jobs of specialists whilst maintaining links with colleagues with a similar background and training. There is one potential hazard. Having two bosses is a departure from classical management principles of clearly defined responsibilities (although the nuclear family is managed on a two boss system). This is not a major disadvantage if the relationships between the two bosses is good. If they are in conflict, the effect on their unfortunate subordinates can be devastating. When this happens, we need to dust down the 'building intergroup cooperation' workshop, and start to manage that problem.

Supervisors as team leaders

In this chapter we have referred to the importance of 'teams' on a number of occasions, and have made fairly elaborate claims for the potential of team work for motivating individuals, integrating tasks and maximising flexibility. Yet we have never defined precisely what we mean by a team, nor have we discussed the principles of group dynamics which give theoretical validation of the potency of groups. The reason for these omissions is simply that this book is not about the principles of group dynamics; it is about developing a committed culture. The topic of group dynamics, however, is important, and any manager who wishes to adopt group working should familiarise himself with the principles involved. The object of this book is to put the case that work can, with time, effort and careful management, be organised on team principles, and that team work is effective. To achieve this objective it is better to give practical examples of what work teams look like, rather than theoretical analysis of principles. If the reader's appetite is whetted, he will continue his study of the subject elsewhere.

For these reasons this section takes an example of the supervisor and describes the differences between the tasks performed by a traditional supervisor in a typical Western 'role' organisation, and the tasks performed by a supervisor in the same organisation after it has, through organisation development, transformed itself to an organisation based on team principles.

Before transformation

In predevelopment company X the supervisor was given production targets by his boss. These targets were in terms of the number of components or assemblies the operators in his section were to produce. He would then allocate the operators to the different machine tools or work stations to ensure that the necessary activity took place so that the targets were met. If he had been in the job for some time, each of his operators would have developed a routine and he would only have to take action if a problem occurred: a machine breaks down, or raw material fails to arrive from stores, or operators fail to arrive at work. He would see himself very much as a problem solver; as the person the operators would come to if they had any difficulties. He was also the person who was blamed by the boss if things went wrong.

Finance department sent him weekly figures that told him about his performance. The supervisor did not trust these figures, and kept detailed records of his own. He spent a lot of his time sitting in his office working on his production figures and used to get annoyed when he was disturbed and asked to deal with a problem on the shopfloor. The system measured everything related to the section's production. Not only the amount produced, but also the number of hours it took, the amount of waste, and energy used, the utilisation of the machine tools, the amount of work in progress, the number of parts rejected by the quality inspector and many other things. The supervisor felt that whatever he did he was measured against, and whatever he achieved was not good enough. He heartily disliked the quality inspector who regularly rejected a shift's production. Although the parts were technically out of specification they both knew they would work in practice and could have been passed.

The supervisor got on well with his operators, although relationships were not close. They gave him little aggravation, and he left them alone as long as they did the job. He believed most of the people came to work only for the wage packet and got little satisfaction from their jobs – how could they, the jobs were boring and repetitive. He had had to work with shop stewards who were a real nuisance and made life difficult by insisting that even the most trivial parts of the labour agreement were followed, but the supervisor's relationship with most of the shop stewards was good, and together they were usually able to work amicably through any problems the operators were having.

The supervisor also got on quite well with his manager, despite his endless demands for more production at less cost. The boss never seemed to be satisfied. The department had a half-hour daily production meeting attended by all the supervisors and chaired by the manager. The supervisor felt that the meeting did not achieve much other than provide him with information. It tended to finish up with the manager giving a lecture and blaming everyone but himself for missed targets.

Once a month the foreman had a meeting with all his operators to go through the set of notes provided by the plant manager to keep all the people informed on the company's overall performance and future plans. He also took this opportunity to keep the section informed about their own production levels and how they had done against the various targets. The operators seemed more interested in this latter information than the company briefing notes. The supervisor believed that keeping his operators informed was important but suspected that many of the operators felt that the meeting was an opportunity for a skive.

After transformation

The post development company X supervisor does a very different job, and he has a very different routine. At the beginning of the shift he attends a meeting of all the operators. The meeting is chaired by one of the operators and the supervisor sits at the back. The meeting begins with a report from a member of the last shift on what they had achieved and what difficulties they had. The days production is the next item on the agenda, and the operators jointly decide on the allocation of work for the day. One of the operators objects when he is allocated to a machine. He has to put together the monthly report on absenteeism for personnel. His job is reallocated. The meeting then hears a report from another operator who has been asked to look into material supply problems. The meeting is not satisfied with what they hear and feel that the stores are not being cooperative. They ask their supervisor to invite the stores supervisor to the next meeting. He agrees. During the meeting the supervisor is brought into the conversation on a number of occasions. His advice is sought and he is asked for information. The supervisor notes that one of the operators seems moody and has made a number of negative comments. Today's meeting lasts half an hour, which is rather longer than usual.

The supervisor has a weekly meeting with his manager and the department's support specialists. This meeting lasts all morning. The first part of this meeting consists of the manager going through production targets. The supervisor notes the production levels that his team are expected to achieve. The meeting then spends ten minutes brainstorming the issues that need to be dealt with in order to improve the department's effectiveness. Priorities are then set and the action needed discussed. The atmosphere is positive and people seem willing, even anxious, to offer their services to find solutions to problems. During the last hour of the meeting the manager outlines some of his, and the company's, long-term plans. He asks for the views of all the people at the meeting, and seems to be listening to what he is being told.

The day after the department meeting the supervisor has his weekly targets meeting with his operators. He chairs this meeting. He informs the team of the production levels expected by the manager during the following week. They discuss if these targets will give them any problems. A number of difficulties will be pointed out, but most of the targets will be agreed. The supervisor listens to the difficulties and agrees an action plan to overcome them. In some cases he will ask for specialist help, in others he will talk to other supervisors, in yet others he will go to his manager and explain why targets cannot be met. The boss will grumble, and ask why but he will accept the decisions of the team. The boss now believes that the team is motivated to meet targets and if they say that a target cannot be met, they have a good reason. The manager and supervisor will talk about how, in the long run they can overcome the problems that are causing the team's inability to meet the company's production needs.

The supervisor allocates one-half day per week to counselling. He meets with each member of his team at least once every six months. They discuss the operator's performance, opinions, ambitions, development plans and any problems he is having at work. They agree an action plan that will lead to increased knowledge and skill, and which will help satisfy the operator's needs for growth and satisfaction at work.

The supervisor spends at least one day in the average week coaching or training his operators. The operators now do many of the jobs that were previously done by either the supervisor or a specialist, such as ensuring the safety regulations are kept to, liaising with maintenance, moving raw materials, collecting personnel statistics, collecting production statistics. This has meant that they have had to be trained in many new skills. The supervisor feels that training seems to be the thing on which he spends most of his time. When the idea of group working was first introduced he himself went on two weeks' training, and then spent most of the next three months organising training for the operators in the knowledge and skills needed to operate in the new way. On the other hand he no longer has to bother about training operators in machine skills – they train each other.

After many months the team concept seems to be working more smoothly. Certainly he is amazed at the change in attitude. No-one now talks about demarcation, people seem to want to pull together and they take a pride in the team's achievement. Not everyone feels comfortable working in teams. Three operators left the company and he has had to spend a lot of his time with two others who do not contribute at the meetings, and who reduce morale by their negative comments.

The supervisor is relieved that the quality standards have remained high. He was pleased to see the back of that quality inspector, but was sceptical about trusting the operators to be responsible for their own quality. However, central quality department's audit shows no reduction in standard; if anything quality has improved. The operators are now much more quality-conscious, and regularly call in the quality engineer to help them with problems. They have appointed one of their members as an internal quality auditor, and he is even tougher than the old inspector.

After several months the union are taking less of an interest in what is going on. At first they were very curious and nosy. Some shop stewards were hostile, but most were cooperative. They seemed to know what it was all about, and were prepared to go along with it. Now they seem to have turned their attention to other things, but the supervisor feels that the union is supporting the principles of team work.

After many months of developing the new system the supervisor will be able to look back at the differences between his old job and his new. The main differences will be:

1. He no longer spends his time dealing with endless day-to-day problems. Now the operators seem to be able to handle these problems themselves, calling in specialist help when they feel they need it. At first the supervisor felt resentful at being bypassed, but that feeling passed after a few months.
2. He no longer feels bogged down with paperwork and recording statistics. It took a long time to train the operators to keep and coordinate their own records, but now everything is going smoothly.
3. He seems to be much more involved in planning and thinking about how to do things better in the long term. His boss takes him into his confidence more, and he feels he has influence on management thinking.
4. Whereas before he often felt he was seen as an ogre, he now feels like a Dutch uncle. He spends a lot of his time smoothing over relationships between people, and helping his group work together as a team. He likes this new role but finds it difficult.
5. In the old days he always felt in charge. Now the team take many of the decisions he used to make, often without bothering to consult him. He feels that he no longer knows everything that is going on, and this makes him feel uncomfortable. It seems that he is now more of a servant to the operators than their boss: finding them the materials needed to do their new jobs (even the paper clips) and working behind the scenes to smooth over the relationships with the other work teams, with whom they seem to be quarrelling all the time.
6. Probably the biggest difference is the amount of time he spends with the operators in a one-to-one relationship. He now spends several hours every week in counselling, training and coaching. Before he would not have had time for all this individual work and would not have seen it as worthwhile. Now he is convinced that the emphasis on the growth of individuals and their jobs pays handsome dividends in work attitudes and commitment. He knows his people much better, feels closer to them and considers some as personal friends.

There is no doubt in the supervisor's mind that the changes have been for the better. He has had to learn a lot and change his own style and attitudes. Some of his old colleagues have been unable to make the adjustment. They have either left the company or been found other jobs within the company. They feel rejected and resentful and he tries to avoid them. Now after many months the benefits of the new ways have become clear and it has been worth all the effort.

Summary and conclusions

Chapter Four makes recommendations for the introduction of new structures before the involvement of the organisation members in the organisation development programme. These changes reduce the levels of hierarchy and introduced business structures. This chapter recommends further restructuring, but these changes should take place in consultation with the people affected and as part of an on-going organisation development programme.

The changes proposed in both this chapter and Chapter Four are important if the committed organisation is to be achieved. The way an organisation is structured has a major effect on how people are managed, the effectiveness of the communication system, and the amount of individual involvement in decision making. Developing the right structures is a necessary part of our organisation development programme.

An organisation being designed from scratch on a green field site can incorporate these ideas comparatively easily. Because the ideas would be novel to most prospective members in this new organisation a great deal of training would be necessary, but given good planning, determination, and understanding at the top our new organisation could operate these principles from the beginning. A mature organisation like company X takes much more time and effort to change. The achievement of a fully autonomous work group would represent the culmination of a great deal of organisation development activity over many years. Given time, understanding, determination and patience it can be (and has been) achieved.

Organisation restructuring is one of a number of aspects of organisation development which must take place at the same time, and which must be complementary to each other. A successful design change must be accompanied by workshop activities, personnel systems development, the development of new management practices and principles and a host of action planning and problem solving sessions. The headman directing an organisation development programme is like a juggler trying to keep half-a-dozen balls in the air at the same time. One falls and his act is in ruins. The timing of any changes in organisation design therefore must be very carefully managed. Some changes must take place before any workshop activities. Operator work teams, on the other hand, should wait for the achievement of a high level of organisation readiness through workshop and other activities before they are introduced. An attempt to introduce team structures where the management are uncommitted or unaware, the union in opposition or the payment system designed to support more traditional work methods, would be doomed. Some parts of the organisation will be ready before others. New organisation designs must be introduced when and where it makes sense. The important thing is to have a clear vision of the developed organisation, and to fit the pieces of the jigsaw whenever and wherever the opportunities become available.

11 Communications

During the late 1970s the Opinion Research Centre (ORC)* published the results of a survey into the attitudes of a randomly selected sample of 2,000 British employees. The survey included a variety of questions about peoples' jobs, frustrations, ambitions and many other things. The findings suggested to many people's surprise that the British employee is in general satisfied with his job, his employer and his conditions of employment.

One question on the survey investigated the priorities of workers; what they most wanted to achieve. Every employee interviewed was shown seventeen cards each with a statement on it. Each statement represented an achievement or objective. By selecting two of these statements, each respondent identified his (or her) highest priorities. The answer came out loud and clear: 26 per cent of the sample chose: 'More information from the top on what is happening and why'. This was the employee's highest priority, higher than more pay, better incentives, more say in running the company, better working conditions, more interesting work, or any of the other seventeen items. The survey results illustrate that good communications are important to employees and that most employees do not feel they have it.

The Japanese believe open, honest and comprehensive communications are essential. Senior supervisors are made responsible for keeping their people informed on all matters that are relevant to their day-to-day work activities, and on any other matters that are of

---

* ORC, *What About the Workers*, Dragonfly Publications Ltd, 1977

interest. Western managers also express the belief that communications are important, but do not seem to give the maintenance of an effective communication system the same priority as do their Japanese opposite numbers. The theme of this chapter is that effective communications are essential for the development and maintenance of a committed culture. We must give to communications the same priority as do the Japanese.

The reason usually given by management for having effective communications is that keeping people informed helps them do their job. People need to have an understanding of where their tasks fit into the overall picture, and they need feedback on how successfully they are performing. These are good reasons, but they are not the only, nor perhaps the most important reason for having effective communications. Good communication is necessary to build trust. Trust is a prerequisite for commitment.

All human beings have a strong need to understand their environment. If they have this understanding they can predict what will happen and so manage their lives more effectively. To understand our environment we need to have information about it. Without this information we feel uncomfortable because we cannot understand or influence events. This need for information is strong in all of us, and if the need is not being met through official communication channels, it will be met by unofficial methods. Telex operators, computer programmers, secretaries are well placed to access information. Their information is usually partial, but that does not stop them founding a good rumour. Where formal communication is bad people develop expertise in interpreting (often correctly) the most obscure pieces of information rather like the Kremlin watchers who are able to interpret the developments in the Politburo power struggles from who is sitting at the top table during formal dinners. The problem is not that the communication generated through unofficial procedures is inaccurate or distorted, but that the need for an unofficial communication system reflects the fact that managers are unwilling or unable to communicate themselves to their people. Organisations where the members feel 'they're holding back again' or 'they don't tell us what is going on' tend to be characterised by suspicion, rumour, distortion, animosity, and mistrust of management's reasons for keeping things to themselves. Such an organisation would not be capable of generating a culture characterised by a high level of commitment. Developing good communications is essential in order to generate trust, cooperation, commitment and the feeling of belonging, and therefore must form part of our organisation development programme.

This chapter is about how to develop a communication system that is open, honest and relevant.

Communication systems

There is no one way to design a communication system. Whilst all organisations should have effective communications, the best way of achieving this objective will vary from one organisation to another. Some small companies with close interpersonal relations, (such as Handy's task cultures) may not need any formal system. Large bureaucracies may require a centralised and systematised communications programme. Organisations where the members are geographically dispersed may need the use of sophisticated modern communication technology – videos, VDU's. Each organisation must decide on how best to communicate to its own members. Many large 'role' organisations use the briefing system pioneered by the Industrial Society.

This system can be a sound base for effective communication. Information that the top management wishes to pass on to the members of the organisation is summarised and published as briefing notes. The senior manager develops the themes in the briefing notes at a presentation to his managers. The managers then make a presentation to their subordinates and provide them with a copy of the notes. Each level briefs the level below, until finally the supervisors brief the operator work groups.

Through this process each work group is provided with regular (usually monthly) information by their immediate supervisor or manager, who answers any questions the group may wish to ask. Company newspapers, and notice boards may supplement this system. A typical two-way briefing system is described in Appendix Five but this system must be modified to meet individual organisation needs. This chapter suggests ways in which companies mught go about developing or improving their system to meet their own particular needs, but no blueprint can be given of an 'ideal' system.

Why so many organisations communicate badly

We have already suggested that the average organisation member gives a high priority to good communications, but only rarely does he feel his needs are being met. Most managers pay lip service to good communications: they are never against them in principle. Many managers, however, are reluctant communicators – particularly when the news is bad. There are three reasons commonly given by the reluctant manager for not passing on information. This section suggests that none of these 'excuses' are really legitimate and that the real reason lies elsewhere. The three excuses often given for poor communications are:

1 'Information given to the shopfloor will be used against us by the union when it comes to negotiations.' Chapter Nine deals with this point in some detail. The essential message of that chapter is that the only way the union can be brought to an understanding of the long-term needs of their members is to develop their understanding of the strategic decisions needed to ensure the organisation progresses. When they can see the broad picture, they will come to view all of the organisation members as being in the same lifeboat; they will become more concerned with the ability of the organisation to provide long-term employment, less concerned with this year's settlement. Open communications will, in the short run, make life more difficult for negotiators (which is why personnel departments are often the most secretive). In the long run it becomes less and less likely as levels of trust improve for the union to use information given to them by management to reinforce bargaining points. UK based Japanese companies tend to have open communications with their unions, and have effective industrial relations. It is difficult to collect concrete evidence on the relationship between open communications, good industrial relations and ability to manage organisation change, but if the thesis presented in this book is correct, they should be close.

If an organisation deliberately sets out to open up its communications it should expect a traumatic period while the union uses its new bargaining power in the traditional battles (the price of poor communication in the past). After that there will be a slow but accelerating improvement in the employee relations climate as trust develops. The transition requires a determination to manage the short-term battles for the long-term peace agreement. The excuse that 'they will use it against us' therefore is only valid in the short run, and leads to practices that will inhibit long-term organisation development.

2 'Information passed on to employees will be used by competitors to the disadvantage of the company.' This excuse is frequently given, but rarely substantiated. Members of competing organisations know a great deal about each other and would learn little from even the most open and honest communications designed to provide employees with information they need or information of interest to them. There will, however, be some occasions when withholding information can be justified for this reason. In an organisation with high trust levels, explanations by senior management that they are not willing to communicate on a topic, and why, will be accepted. Organisations where managers use commercial security as an

excuse for not communicating, will not develop these high trust levels. In these organisations, the excuse will not be accepted.

3 'The more you give, the more they demand'. This is very true. People have an almost insatiable appetite for information on topics that are important to them. If managers are committed to open communications they will be spending a great deal of their time managing the communication process. If they want a committed workforce, this is one of the penalties they must pay. If they themselves believe that their time and effort will be more than compensated for in the long run, they will give communications the necessary priority.

In an organisation determined to change towards a culture where all are committed to working together to identify and solve problems, to plan actions for improvements and to achieve high levels of flexibility, open communications are essential. Our three common excuses only rarely provide a satisfactory reason for not communicating, and managers can often be persuaded of their lack of validity. There are, however, three other causes of bad communications that, although rarely publicly given as an excuse, are more pervasive in causing poor performance in this critical area.

1 'If no-one knows what I am doing, I cannot get found out'. If we are open and honest with others we cannot hide our own personal limitations, and our mistakes are revealed for all to see. Open communications cannot take place in an organisation where members (particularly senior members) are not prepared to provide information which would show themselves, or their team, in a bad light. Indeed, in such organisations, senior members may be actively generating false information which will show them or their teams in the best possible light. Organisation members can be highly creative when directing their talents towards generating data against which they are being evaluated.

The Japanese, when asked to comment on the cultural differences between themselves and Western organisations, particularly point out the Westerner's tendency to sweep problems under the corporate carpet. To the Japanese problems are to be brought into the full light of day so that they can be understood and action taken to put them right. Problems must be revealed for all to see, so that all can learn and all can contribute towards the search for a better way of doing things. They believe that only then can the organisation progress.

If we are to move an organisation towards more honest and open communications, we must first of all produce an atmosphere where the members feel comfortable about revealing their faults and problems. If the atmosphere is one where people are striving for higher standards, where they are evaluated for their achievements of these higher standards, and where mistakes are seen as an opportunity for learning rather than an excuse to lay blame, communications will become more open. In organisations where people are evaluated for their ability to give their boss a quiet life, and where they are remembered not for their achievements, but for their blunders, communications will become more secretive. Senior management set the example by rewarding achievements rather than punishing errors. Then their people will not feel vulnerable if communications become more open and honest.

2 Effective communications are hard work. Communication systems require maintenance, feedback and commitment. So do individual communications from the boss to the subordinate. To be effective each member of an organisation must keep in mind that he has information that others need or want. He must actively share it by doing something. Many organisation members are poor communicators, not because they do not see the importance of keeping people informed, but because they are too lazy to think about the information needs of others, or too lacking in empathy to appreciate what those needs are.

3 Effective communications need skill. Effective communication frequently requires that the communicator formally addresses others in large groups where he is asked questions which may be difficult or embarassing to answer. Many organisation members simply do not have the skills or the self-confidence to do this well. This is a common problem, but if the rest of the system is right, it is not difficult to overcome. Properly designed and run training courses can be very effective in improving people's ability and confidence in making presentations.

There are a number of reasons, therefore, why many organisations do not communicate effectively, even though there is a belief possibly backed up by formal policy statements, in having an effective system. Management will always find excuses in these organisations for not communicating well, but the reasons are likely to be, they are punished for doing so, they are not prepared to give communications a high enough priority, or they feel inadequate to the task. It is up to the senior management to identify and manage any blockages.

This next section should help them to look in the right places to identify those blockages.

Improving communications in company X

The management planning workshop and the management principles workshop have taken place and the programme of supervisor and specialist workshop has started. One of the products of the workshops has been an appreciation of the importance of good communications on the part of management. They were pleased that they had had a monthly briefing group system for a number of years and that it appeared to be working well.

The plant manager liked to spend half an hour each morning at 'the sharp end' – usually on the shopfloor. It helped him, as he put it, 'to get a feel for what is really going on'. From his conversations with operators, he became concerned that the information he was incorporating in his briefing notes either was not filtering down, or was filtering down only in a distorted form. He asked the operators why they felt they were not being kept informed. They felt the supervisors were to blame and described them as uninterested and uncommitted to the communication system.

The plant manager was concerned about what he heard. He remembered that the supervisors had never received any systematic training in operating the system even though it had been in place for five years. He told the consultant, retrained to assist with the organisation development programme, that he intended to ask his staff trainer to design and run a programme to increase the supervisor's knowledge and skill in operating the briefing group system.

The consultant listened to the plant manager and then took the first opportunity to talk to some supervisors. What he heard from them led him to advise the plant manager to take a different course of action. He suggested to the plant manager that before arranging a training programme he should find out in more detail what the problems were. The plant manager accepted this suggestion and decided that the investigation would provide a useful project for one of the company's younger graduate trainees. The consultant briefed the trainee, and suggested that he concentrated his investigation on the supervisors. The consultant also helped the trainee to develop his understanding of survey techniques, questionnaire design, and interviewing skills. A timetable for the finished report was agreed.

When the report was completed it became clear that the investigator had found himself in a hornet's nest. He reported that the supervisors felt a high level of threat and discomfort with their role in the communications system. The main points the report made were that:

1 Supervisors did not themselves understand the information on the briefing notes, and they felt threatened because they could

not answer questions. A major annoyance was that the briefing notes were full of abbreviations understood only by management (and not understood by all of them).

2 The form of presentation and the content of the briefing notes varied from month-to-month, which made people suspicious that things were deliberately left out in months where the news was bad.

3 Both they and the operators found them boring; they did not provide information about the things in which they were interested.

4 The supervisor frequently was himself only briefed by his manager just before he had to make his presentation to his operators; he did not have time to prepare.

5 The briefing notes were supposed to come with visual aids; these frequently did not arrive, or the overhead projector was broken or 'borrowed', or the room pre-booked.

6 The union representatives had been briefed previously by the plant manager; they frequently knew more than the supervisor, and were able to embarrass him by demonstrating the supervisor's lack of knowledge.

7 Many operators were reluctant to attend the monthly briefing meetings because they saw them as irrelevant, because they could not get answers to questions, and because much of the content was unintelligible to them; the supervisors found it difficult to generate discussion.

8 Shopfloor supervisors were evaluated on the percentage of the time that their machines were producing. Time taken at briefing meetings reduced this percentage which meant that the supervisors were motivated to spending as little time as possible at briefing groups.

The report concluded that as a result of these problems supervisors felt vulnerable, unsupported, and hostile towards the top management who had introduced the system. The plant manager was somewhat shocked by the report, and agreed that any training programme should be delayed until at least some of these problems were resolved. His first reaction was to restrict this rather damaging report to managers, but it did not take long to persuade him that given the nature of the report's subject matter and his overall organisation development objectives he really ought, when the time was right, to make it available to all organisation members. Once the report was made public, the plant manager was under extra pressure to see that something was done about it.

The plant manager and the consultant had a discussion on what steps should be taken to put things right. Based on this discussion the consultant put together some concrete proposals. The plant manager sent the proposals, together with the report to the senior managers. He asked them to consult with their department managers and to discuss the results of these consultations with him at a board meeting.

At this board meeting the senior managers said that they recognised the problems the supervisors were having, and felt that they had some of the same problems themselves. The action proposed was welcomed, but they did take the opportunity to propose some minor modifications to reflect their particular circumstances.

It was clear that all the management team was committed to good communications, and would support, with some modifications, the proposals that had been developed. These proposals were then actioned. The main action points were:

1 The young graduate who had prepared the report was given the responsibility, working directly for the plant manager, of preparing the monthly briefing notes. He was given the job title of communications assistant and was expected:
   (*a*) To take the information that the plant manager wanted to communicate and translate it to a message that would be understood.
   (*b*) To inform the plant manager of the information needs of the different parts of the organisation and ensure the information was relevant.
   (*c*) To develop visual aids that could be used by the managers and supervisors to support their presentations.
   (*d*) To provide an information service; he became a resource to which people could turn for reliable information.
2 Managers and supervisors were expected to include matters of more local interest, and were given support by the communication assistant in preparing this material.
3 A 'request for information' system was introduced, where any member of the organisation could, through the manager or supervisor running the briefing group, ask for information. This request was routed through the communications assistant to the person with the information, who was expected to respond within five days.

One effect of those changes was an increasing belief on the part of all the people in the company that there was a real effort to inform, a more knowledgeable workforce, and a management and supervisory group who felt more comfortable operating the system. This resulted in a marked (and measurable) increase in trust and cooperation. This effect began within six months and continued to grow with the development of the improved system for two years.

Another result of the review of the communications system was a demand, particularly from supervisors, for training in presentation skills. Once they were comfortable with the system, they wanted to operate it as effectively as possible. The organisation was now ready for the training programme that had been the plant manager's first reaction to his realisation that all was not well with the communication system.

There was one additional bonus that came through this approach to improving communications. The communication assistant's role was an ideal vehicle for management development. To do his job well he needed to have his finger on the pulse of each part of the organisation. He needed to spend a lot of his time talking with shopfloor people in order to discover how effective the briefing system was, and how it could be improved. His job involved access to all levels including the plant manager and his senior management, and also involved a need to gain an understanding of all aspects of the organisation. As the communication system matured, people seen as having management development potential were allocated to this role for a six-month period.

Principles of effective communications

The previous section described how company X developed its communications so that the system was able to complement the other organisation development activities. Without an effective communication system, the workshop activities and the organisational restructuring would have been insufficient to develop the committed culture which is the aim of the programme. The previous section is designed to provide an illustration of how the principles of good communications work in practice. This section lists those principles:

Custom-build the system

Each organisation has information needs to meet that are different from those found in other organisations. The communication system must therefore be tailor-made for each organisation to ensure that those specific needs are met. In designing a system, what goes on elsewhere can be used as a guide or model. The 'monthly briefing group' system will have relevance for most 'role' type organisations, for instance. But whatever blueprint is chosen it must be adapted. The way to ensure this adaptation is to systematically investigate how the system is currently working, define the problems, and take action to put them right.

Use a problem solving approach

If communications are bad, people will not know about it: if they know about it, the communications cannot be bad! Communication systems, more than any other, require a great deal of maintenance. To ensure this maintenance takes place, the system must have built into itself systematic feedback about the problems people are having. This feedback will allow action to be identified that will ensure continuous fine-tuning of the system.

Ensure communication is two-way

Most communication systems emphasise top manager's informing the lower levels. The communication system should be about communications between all levels in the organisation. There is a need for people at the lower levels to be kept informed about the organisation's performance and plans, but senior people should also have the opportunity to receive information on the attitudes, concerns and behaviour of the people 'at the sharp-end'. This is difficult to do systematically. In company X before the system was improved, it was achieved through two processes: the plant manager spending time talking to operators, and a 'one-off' investigation of the supervisor's views on the working of the system. Effective, two-way communications require a more systematic approach. Attitude surveys are a frequently used technique for generating upward communications. Two-way communications can be built into a 'monthly briefing group' system (see Appendix Five).

Adapt the message to the recipient

Every communication has a generator and a receiver. If the receiver is incapable of accepting the message, no communication has taken place. In company X the people to whom the communications were directed did not understand it and were not interested in it. The message might have been precise and accurate, it might have reflected what the plant manager wanted the organisation members to know about, but it never became a communication. There was a generator but no receiver.

The message must take into account the background knowledge, educational standards and interests of the recipient. Feedback on the reaction of the receivers to the message can allow the 'generators' to fine-tune their message to ensure that it gets through.

Involve the recipients in the message

Adults are not empty vessels into which information can be poured. They evaluate the message: does it make sense; do I trust the originator of the message; what are they not telling us; what do the people with whom I work think about it; what does my boss think about it? Their acceptance or rejection of the message depends on whether they feel comfortable with it. To help them make these judgements they need to bounce their ideas off others, especially people who share their background and interests, at discussion groups where people are encouraged to exchange views on what they thought of the message. If these discussions are to be successful, the participants need to be encouraged to ask questions and to clarify anything that is not clear to them. These discussions will help the person towards whom the message is directed to understand it better, judge its meaningfulness, and decide if it makes sense to him. If it passes all three tests, he will internalise it. He will also remember it better.

Train the communicators

Many people find making presentations to groups of people stressful, others can take it in their stride. Making presentations requires confidence and skill. Training can provide both, and if effectively run, also increase commitment to the importance of working the communication system effectively. A training programme designed to increase knowledge, skills and commitment would incorporate:

1 A presentation on the reasons for the company's communication system, and how the system operates.
2 Practice in making presentations, with feedback, ideally using video.
3 Identification of trainee problems, and discussion of action to overcome them.
4 Instruction in the preparation and use of visual aids.
5 Commitment by each trainee to action to improve his own performance.

Use visual aids

Visual aids can be a real boon to effective communication. Even key words projected on an overhead projector, or written on a blackboard can focus the audience's attention, and organise the presentation.

Reward effective communications

If management want the organisation's communications to be effective they should make the achievement of good communication one of the things against which their subordinates are evaluated. They should monitor levels of performance, and recognise real achievements (there is no suggestion here that the reward should be monetary).

Ensure top management support

Top management support is needed for all organisation development activities, including the development and maintenance of the communication system.

Make the communications system one person's responsibility

This is the last principle, but is certainly not the least. It is considered last because it relates to all the others.

The role of the communication assistant is to:

1 Provide feedback information on the way the system is working; this information to be the basis for action to:
   (*a*) Develop the system so that it meets the organisation's needs.
   (*b*) Manage any problems people are having.
   (*c*) Ensure the message is understood and relevant to the recipient.
2 Assist the plant manager and other senior managers by collecting relevant information to include in their communications.
3 Develop and distribute visual aids.
4 Train the communicators.

He should not be expected to evaluate the communicator's performance. Evaluation is incompatable with the role of helper and supporter.

Communication systems take a lot of maintenance, and therefore a lot of resources. They do not work effectively unless there is constant feedback on what is happening, and particularly the problems people are having. This feedback will not happen unless one person is clearly identified as being 'Mr. Communication' and he is given the time, support, and resources to do his job.

Summary and conclusions

This chapter has emphasised the importance of open, honest and relevant communications in developing an organisation culture characterised by trust and commitment. Organisation members have a strong need to know about and understand their working environment. This need can only be met by management giving priority to developing and maintaining an effective communication system. Failure to communicate leads to an organisation whose cultural characteristics are rumour, suspicion, distortion and distrust.

There are a number of reasons why communications tend to be poor in many Western organisations. The principles reasons are:

1 Organisations do not reward openness and effective communication skills.
2 Good communication is time-consuming and managers give other responsibilities higher priority over maintaining effective communication systems.
3 Good communications require high levels of skill, and organisations do not give priority to the training necessary to ensure communicators have these skills.

If there is no commitment to good communications, managers will readily find excuses for avoiding making the effort.

There are a number of principles or rules that must be followed if an organisation is to have an effective communication system. These principles are:

1 The system must be tailor-made to ensure that it meets the organisation's needs: there is no one best way to communicate.
2 The system should be maintained through a problem solving approach: define the problem, develop proposals for solutions, implement proposals. The problem solving approach requires systematic investigation to provide information on what is happening, and management commitment to providing time and resources.
3 Communication should be two-way, so that all organisation members understand what is going on at all levels.
4 The message must take into account the knowledge, interest and motivation of the recipient.
5 The recipient should be given the opportunity, through discussion with his peers, of evaluating the message.
6 Communicators should be given the necessary skills and confidence through training.
7 Visual aids help to ensure interest and understanding.
8 Openness and good communication skills should be rewarded.
9 Top management should be committed.
10 One person should be given the responsibility for supporting the communication system.

Some of these rules are more important than others, but if they are broken a lot of wasted effort can be put into attempts to communicate that are doomed to failure.

Good communication is one of the most important yet underestimated ingredients needed for developing a committed culture.

12 Support for the Organisation Development Process

The responsibility for the organisation development programme must always clearly be seen as belonging to the headman. He must have the vision, the drive, the determination and the leadership qualities to guide the organisation, over a number of years, towards the changes in culture that will achieve the committed workforce and a flexible and efficient organisation. He cannot, however, manage such a far reaching, and at times traumatic change process without help and support.

Chapter Eleven discussed the need for an individual to be allocated the responsibility for supporting the communication process. In that chapter it was argued that effective communications are necessary to build an atmosphere of trust, and trust is one of the necessary conditions for a committed organisation. Communications are sufficiently important to warrant the allocation of resources to support the development process. In this chapter, support in two other areas is discussed. The following section discusses organisation development consultancy, and suggests that the headman will usually need someone with technical expertise to provide him with advice and guidance and to manage the day-to-day change programme he is leading. The last section emphasises the high demand for training that is generated by the organisation development programme and which must be satisfied if the change programme is to succeed. Some ways of meeting these training needs are suggested.

The organisation development consultant

All headmen must have a clear vision of what the organisation will be like at the end of the organisation development programme, of the resources needed over a period of years to support the programme, and of their own role in the change process. Most headmen will not have the specialist knowledge or skills, or the time to manage the day-to-day issues that are generated by a complex organisation development programme. They will therefore need the help and support of someone who can act as guide and adviser and who will also manage, administer, and monitor the process. The need is for a person with technical skills who works directly for the headman in order to assist him to meet his objectives. This is a consultant rather than a management role. The consultant may be an outsider, or an internal appointment. He would carry out the following tasks to support the organisation development programme:

1. Advise the headman on all aspects of the organisation development programme: communications, personnel systems, workshop designs, training, organisation design, union relationships, team development, job redesign.
2. Run workshop activities: plan programmes, define objectives, clarify roles of participants and ensure that workshops are successful by recognising problems and pitfalls and taking steps to avoid them.
3. Provide an organisation measurement service through questionnaires, surveys or action research to assess the effects and effectiveness of the change programme.
4. Stimulate and integrate all the action that needs to be taken to implement the organisation development (OD) programme.
5. Train the organisation members in the skills needed to operate in the new organisation environment.

The OD consultant's job has a number of unique characteristics. His role is different from most consultant roles in the following ways:

1. Although he should be an expert in his field (which usually means a qualification in behavioural science and a number of year's experience), he should avoid the temptation of advising people on what decisions to make. The headman and his managers should make the decisions, the OD consultant should help them think through the alternatives before the decisions are made. The consultant might know about OD, but only the manager knows about his people, his problems and his organisation, so over reliance on the consultant can be dangerous. On

the other hand the consultant is there to help implement decisions made by managers.

2 The OD consultant should be seen as expert, approachable and 'neutral' by all the organisation members. He must be acceptable to managers, supervisors, specialists, operators and union officials – a daunting prospect. All members of the organisation must see him as a resource they can use.

3 The OD consultant concentrates on the 'process' of management decision making within the organisation. He is less concerned with the quality of a decision being made (whether or not it is the right decision), than he is with who makes the decisions; who is consulted, who is left out.

4 The OD consultant is something of an anarchist – he acts as an outsider questioning the values and assumptions of the people with the responsibility to get things done, and asking if there is a better way. He has the outsiders capacity for overview, he is not trapped into the values and politics of the organisation, and because he has little to lose, he will be willing to confront top management.

5 The OD consultant working in an organisation must clarify exactly who he is working for: who his client is. This is not always as obvious as it seems. When he is having preliminary discussions on an assignment with a manager whose opening comments are 'The boss feels we have a problem and I am told you are someone who can help us solve it', the danger bells should ring. Does the manager agree that it is a problem? Does he resent being told to bring in an outsider? The OD consultant must clarify these points, must make it clear to the person to whom he is talking that the only way he can work as a consultant is for his client to believe that he can be helped by him. If the manager feels he has been pressured, or is resentful, he will do his best to demonstrate to his boss that bringing in outsiders was a waste of time and money. That way he will prove his boss wrong. There are many ways that the manager can ensure that a consultant fails, without actually appearing uncooperative. The consultant needs from his client a continuous flow of information on the subtle personal relationships and communication patterns which are the life blood of an organisation. If the outsider is excluded from the informal system he cannot make the contribution that is expected of him. The wise consultant will know when to turn down an assignment.

Because of these unique characteristics, the successful OD consultant operates in a way that is very different from the management process of most organisation members. He must influence through being seen as expert and helpful rather than because of his formal position. He will be seen as helpful if he can assist organisation members, at all levels, to achieve their goals. If the headman is doing his job properly, those goals will include the achievement of organisation development.

Training

Organisation development means change. Change means that the organisation members will need to master new skills, gain new knowledge, develop new attitudes. New skills, knowledge and attitudes cannot be gained without a systematic programme of training and development for all the members involved in organisation development. In our company X the organisation development programme involved all the members, so all the members became involved in training activities. The organisation change programme therefore required a commitment to training on the part of company X's headman and the allocation of resources to training. Without training the organisation members will not develop the new skills, knowledge and attitudes, and the development programme will not be supported.

The driving force controlling and stimulating the organisation development programme is the series of workshops. One of the objectives of each workshop is to increase the knowledge of the participants, but in addition each generates a demand for further training. In company X these were:

1 The management workshop led to a demand for a greater understanding of the corporate management philosophy and for training in appraisal skills, in coaching and counselling skills, and in management decision making.
2 The supervisor workshop also led to a demand for man-management skills training and in addition to training in communications and for a more detailed understanding of the principles and applications of job redesign, autonomous work groups and quality circles.
3 The specialist workshop led to a demand for training in different branches of engineering so that the people had wider skills, and also to a demand for a greater understanding of manufacturing team designs.
4 The operator workshop led to a demand for training for operators in new machine skills, team working, and managing the extra tasks allocated to teams.
5 The union workshops led to a demand for greater understanding

of all aspects of the change process, and particularly those parts of the programme that would have a major impact on the union members.

The total amount of training generated by the workshop programme was enormous in company X, and required a small team of trainers to be fully occupied over a period of years. As the programme developed and matured, the training emphasis did not become any less great. The developed organisation places great emphasis on the growth of all the organisation's members' skills, knowledge and attitudes in order to achieve flexibility and commitment. The greater the pool of ability, the more easily the organisation can change the tasks it performs. The more committed the organisation members are the more they will be willing to take on new tasks and learn new skills. As our organisation develops, therefore, there will be no reduction in the emphasis in the training and development of the people, but there could well be a changing need for the services of specialist trainers.

One of the objectives of an organisation development programme is to make all organisation members trainers. Managers and supervisors take on more of a trainers role, with an emphasis being put on the development of subordinates. Each operator becomes responsible for training other operators in machine skills. The specialists not only provide support to the manufacturing teams, but also increase the team's independence and self-sufficiency by instructing the other team members in the skills needed to do the job themselves without the need to call in help. Each member of the organisation is responsible for his own growth and the growth of his colleagues, so the specialist trainer will become less concerned with providing a service in these areas. His new role will be to increase the understanding and skills of all the organisation members in effective training techniques. Another key role for trainers in the organisation development programme is to provide comprehensive induction programmes so that new members of the organisation understand the principles on which it works.

The skills of the trainer, and the skills of the workshop consultant or catalyst are similar. Training and organisation development are inter-related in other ways. It could well be sensible in some organisations to have a small unit with responsibility for supporting organisation development and providing training support.

In this section the importance of training to support the organisation development programme is being emphasised. Also emphasised is the need to increase the training and coaching skills of all the organisation members as the organisation development programme advances. Discussion of the techniques of effective training to support organisation change is beyond the scope of this book, although many of these principles are incorporated in the principles for running workshops (pp. 65–74): listening, getting them to think it through for themselves, using problem solving approaches, team building.

13 Personnel Systems and Personnel Departments

Handy describes his 'role' culture as being controlled by rules and procedures. Each part of the organisation's day-to-day activity is controlled by formal and written regulations: job descriptions define the work people do, remuneration systems define their rewards, grievance procedures define the way disputes are handled, labour agreements control the interaction between unions and management, and there are many more. Many of these sets of rules and procedures are highly complex and detailed: the labour agreement could be thirty to forty pages long, job grading could encompass fifteen or more levels of white collar members, and a further eight to ten levels of blue collar. The objective of these regulations is to ensure that the collective wisdom of the organisation is enshrined and passed on from generation to generation, and to ensure that decisions through the organisation are consistent and seen as fair. If people feel grieved it cannot be due to an individual being unfair, because he was only following the rules. If organisation members do not like the rules, there are ways of changing them through agreed procedures (although this of course takes time). This has the effect of developing an organisation climate that is predictable and secure, but the emphasis on rules and procedures, on precedents and regulations, can be frustrating for the individual who wants to do things in new ways, or is power-oriented, or wants control over his work, or is more interested in results than method.

The role culture is successful when the organisation operates in an unchanging environment. Where the market is stable or predictable or where the organisation can control its own environment, rules and procedures and programmed work will be successful. The role culture is, however, always vulnerable. The market may become less predictable or favourable, the organisation may become less able to control its own environment. The role culture will be slow to perceive the need to change, and slow to change even if the need is seen. The rules and regulations will still be followed even when they cease to be relevant, or where adjustments to the environment require much more rapid and creative action than the bureaucratic procedures will allow. Many large organisations found themselves unable to react to the increased tempo of change during the 1970s.

One of the objectives of the organisation development programme is to increase the flexibility of the organisation: its ability to react to changes in the environment. (This flexibility does not require that change should be the norm; if the environment is stable, the organisation should be able to sense this and to continue with its current activities.) The organisation development programme, therefore, must come to terms with the rules and regulations, and with their custodians: the personnel department.

The personnel systems, therefore, are what make role organisations comfortable and predictable, frustrating and inflexible. The organisation development programme wishes to replace frustration with commitment, predictability with flexibility. It must follow that organisation development will decrease the comfort level, and make life more challenging. Individuals will be expected to do more things, master new skills, accept new challenges. They will not be allowed to continue working on the same tasks year after year. The mastery of a task is a good reason to move on to another one and so increase the overall skills and knowledge of individuals, and therefore the pool of talent upon which the organisation can draw. The introduction of experimental job redesign and autonomous work group projects under sheltered agreements will mean that some parts of the organisation will look very different from others, which will lead to conflict and increasing unpredictability. It will also lead to individuals feeling that they no longer know where they stand, and that they are being unfairly treated.

The organisation development programme will require that all the personnel systems are reviewed. For instance:

1 The payment system will have to reflect the fact that people are working in teams: individual bonus or piece work will not complement team working.
2 Flexibility of work within both specialist and shopfloor teams cannot exist alongside restricted individually based job descriptions.

3 Hierarchy cannot be reduced in the presence of job evaluation schemes with many levels, and which emphasise extra payments for direct supervision, deemphasising reward for gaining extra skills.

Every change brought about by the organisation development programme must be complemented by a change in the rules and regulations. Usually this means that the rules become more flexibile, simpler and more open to different interpretations to meet different needs, but in some circumstances new personnel systems may be needed; for example, to support greater participation, for improved communication or to introduce new technology. It is not possible to define what changes will be needed in any one organisation, but it is clear that all organisation change programmes create a lot of work for personnel departments, and some changes in their roles. The impact on the personnel department of company X can be used to illustrate some of these issues, and also some of the dilemmas into which the organisation development puts personnel.

The management principles workshop held in company X resulted in a very glum looking personnel manager. The management group had agreed on a set of principles that would govern the organisation in the future. They were committed to making the necessary structural changes over a period of time to implement these principles. The full implications of these changes on the personnel functions became increasingly clear to the personnel manager. The structural changes would have to be accompanied by changes in payment, in bonus, in job evaluation and grading, and in appraisal and evaluation. His particular chagrin was that the company had recently completed the introduction of a complex and costly job evaluation scheme. This new job evaluation scheme had a heavy weighting for supervisory experience. The management team had just decided that low hierarchy was an important principle to follow if job enrichment and autonomy were to be introduced.

The personnel manager's fears were soon justified. The senior manager responsible for the purchase of capital equipment decided to restructure in line with the new philosophy. Previously he had specialist staff – each an expert in one aspect of the department's overall task and organised on three levels: middle manager, supervisor, engineer. The new organisation reduced the hierarchy to two levels and changed the jobs. In future each member of the department would have identified clients (normally a manufacturing area) and would provide all the services needed by that area. The engineers responded well to the change: they welcomed the opportunity to enrich their jobs, widen their knowledge and develop personal relations with their 'clients'.

They undertook the necessary extra training with enthusiasm. The problem came when the new jobs were evaluated. The system had placed great emphasis on giving credit for supervising people. The new philosophy expected people to be autonomous and managers to have wide spans of control. The result was low grading and high dissatisfaction. The members of the department felt that they had shown flexibility, had been fully cooperative, and had worked hard to ensure the changes worked, and had even reduced their own chances of promotion, yet the company was unwilling or unable to recognise or respond to their needs.

Personnel department was in a real dilemma. Changing systems takes time and money. Personnel departments have limited resources, and cannot always respond, even when they understand and are committed to the need. Yet when things go wrong personnel gets the blame. The people feel that they have been fully cooperative in introducing new ways of working but personnel are being their old bureaucratic selves. Like many of the problems generated by organisation change these dilemmas can only be handled by the person whose job it is to provide the direction, vision, coordination and the integration – the headman. He must ensure that personnel has the knowledge, understanding, resources and commitment to support the changes taking place.

In many ways the objectives of the personnel department are in conflict with organisation development. There is some natural conflict between the organisation development consultant and the personnel manager, particularly if the personnel department is seen (or sees itself) as being responsible for the management of the company's human resources.

Some personnel departments are even called 'human resources departments', but invariably, they do not manage people, they develop and maintain people systems. The job of managing the people belongs to the line manager who relies on personnel for administrative back-up and advice. The advice they give is on how to operate consistently and fairly the company's policies and procedures. An organisation without the need for developed policies and procedures (and this will include most small organisations in the task or power categories) will invariably have either no personnel department, or a small one. The organisations with large and powerful personnel functions are invariably 'role' cultures.

The result of this is that personnel departments are evaluated on their ability to 'keep the lid on' any trouble. Employee relations problems are deemed to be due to a failure on the part of the personnel department, although they frequently have little impact on the events which caused them. For personnel, the best way to head off problems is to develop agreed policies and procedures into which to divert any conflicts. These procedures take the steam out of situations by causing delays and by ensuring that a consistent set of rules are operated. Personnel departments are the arch bureaucrats whose anguished cry of 'Get back into procedure' echoes behind any manager who tries to handle his problems in a new and creative way. Personnel departments are put in a difficult situation when they are expected both to operate a 'steady state' function, and also to facilitate change.

In conclusion, therefore, organisation development requires new and different personnel systems, and it requires that the rules and regulations are more flexible and less restricting. These changes will produce, at least during the transition period, an organisation which is seen by its members as less predictable, less stable, and less consistent. These are the penalties to be paid for increased understanding, flexibility, adaptability and the capacity to react rapidly and effectively to changes in the organisation's environment. Organisation development presents personnel departments with a great deal of work, a more difficult job, and role conflicts with which they must come to terms. The headman must help them by not expecting from personnel department that they are both custodians of the personnel systems and agents for change. That will maximise their conflicts.

14 Conclusions

The central theme of this book is that the successful organisations of the 1980s and 1990s will be those that take active steps to develop a capacity to both manage change and also to pursue an active search for a more effective use of available resources. These organisations will have management willing and able to plan for the achievement of long-term goals, and avoid preoccupation with the day-to-day issues and the short-term problems. These managements will give time to a regular review of:

1 Trends in the organisation's environment.
2 Recurrent problems that are inhibiting progress.
3 Opportunities for increased efficiency.

and they will plan and implement action to:

4 Adapt the organisation to the environment of the future.
5 Solve the recurrent problems.
6 Take advantage of the opportunities.

These managers will appreciate the potential of the untapped human resources within their organisation and will actively work towards developing the skills, knowledge and above all the commitment of all the people to increase the flexibility and efficiency of that part of the organisation, however small, for which they are responsible. The successful organisation of the future can only be achieved through an organisation development programme led by senior management with determination and vision. A practical organisation development programme to achieve the committed company has been proposed.

Perhaps we can be accused of under estimating the difficulties, and skipping over some of the many problems. Certainly, not all the action needed to achieve the committed culture has been spelt out in detail in this book. For instance, there has been little analysis of the resources needed for training to support a change programme. The amount of time and energy needed and the frustrations and set-backs inevitable when introducing job redesign, work group structures or quality circles has not been discussed in detail. Also we have described a change programme in an organisation without violent fluctuations in demand for its products and without a multi-union structure. The change programme will certainly be more difficult if the commercial environment is unpredictable, and if the various interest groups (shareholders, unions, suppliers, customers, local authorities, government) have conflicts of interests that are difficult to reconcile. If the reader has gained the impression that a comprehensive organisation development programme is easy, this is regrettable. There is no doubt that even in the most favourable situation, the changing of attitudes and the development of the skills, knowledge and commitment of the people to achieve more effective and flexible organisations is a daunting task.

The task is essentially to reverse the 'natural' process of bureaucratisation. As organisations mature they tend to develop an administrative system that increases the social and psychological differences between leaders and led. The leaders seek increasing control, develop rules and sanctions, see the led as objects to be treated as extensions of a machine. The organisation development programme aims to give all the organisation members autonomy to influence decisions in their own work areas. In this way their talents will be utilised and their commitment grow. Only by using all the talents available – both human and technological – will our organisation prosper in the highly competitive world that lies ahead.

APPENDICES

Appendix 1 Management Planning Workshop

Introduction

Appendix 1 presents the summaries of the presentations made by management to the headman during the management planning workshop. This workshop is described in Chapter Five. The action plan was used by the headman as the blueprint for a systematic programme of organisation development in company X, although the plans were modified in the light of increasing knowledge and experience.

Advantages and disadvantages of the corporate management philosophy

Advantages

1 Many of the principles had already been accepted and the corporate management philosophy gives support to changes that were already occurring.
2 Change forces people to think long term and plan ahead. It is good to rethink and regroup and to work for a forward thinking company.
3 The new organisation will be better able to meet the challenges of the future.
4 The new management philosophy will improve shopfloor cooperation.
5 The corporate management philosophy has the improvement of quality and productivity as one of its major objectives.

6 The management will accept the challenge of managing the new ways and are developing commitment.
7 Opportunities for the development of employees at all levels are being increased.
8 Working in smaller groups will lead to improvements in industrial relations and communications.
9 The restructuring offers long-term benefits of a streamlined structure, cost savings and increased productivity.

Disadvantages

1 Increasing expectation for reward will result from people being asked to do extra tasks; this expectation may not be met.
2 Managers will be expected to spend more time on long-term planning, but will still be held responsible for short-term problems.
3 Major effort in planning and training needed to support changes: our resources will be stretched.
4 Natural resistance to change will be exposed.
5 End result uncertain: will it lead to increased effectiveness?
6 Major difficulty in managing the people who have no place in the new organisation or who cannot change.
7 New management style will lead to more difficulties imposing the discipline necessary to:
(*a*) Introduce more effective computerised planning;
(*b*) Ensure conformity to health and safety regulations.
8 Lack of consultation with the people involved in the restructuring will lead to lack of understanding and commitment.
9 Union opposition could be generated, which will lead to worsening industrial relations.

Summary

Whilst there are reservations from some managers about whether the plans for the new organisation represents the best way of moving ahead, there was overall agreement that:

1 The disadvantages can be overcome.
2 There is commitment to making it work.

Action plan

Problem	*Action needed*
1 *Management understanding* The management group does not fully understand the ways the corporate management philosophy can be translated into effective local action for improvements.	Hold a further workshop to discuss practical examples of job redesign, job rotation, autonomous working and to study examples within the corporation of the philosophy being practised. Headman to arrange within two months.
2 *Systems* How do we develop the following systems:	
(a) Participation	Invite the unions to form a joint working party to develop proposals. Work to begin by March 19 . . .
(b) Appraisal/work planning	See Management training.
(c) Communications	Establish a working party to review the workings of the current system and recommend improvements. John Smith responsible; to report by June 30th.
(d) Job evaluation	Personnel to develop new systems through the following process: 1 Informal discussions with union 2 Presentation of proposals to managers 3 Agreement of proposals by managers 4 Formal negotiations with unions. Proposals to be developed by August.
(e) Remuneration	As in 2d above.
3 *Management training* In order to operate within the corporate management philosophy the management group will need extra skills and knowledge in:	
(a) Appraisal and work planning	All managers to participate in training activities designed to: 1 Identify modifications to the

Problem	*Action needed*
	current appraisal system needed to complement new philosophy. 2 Develop knowledge and skills to be able to operate new system effectively.
(b) Improving staff effectiveness	Participate in 3a above and also inhouse courses in: 1 Coaching and counselling 2 Delegation and involving staff in decision making. Organisation consultant to develop proposals for consideration by management at the next workshop.
4 *Non-management training* How do we provide specialists, supervision, union and shop-floor employees with the necessary new skills and knowledge.	The first priority should be to 'cascade down' understanding of the corporate management philosophy through workshops. One of the tasks of these workshops should be to identify training needs. Headman to arrange when time considered right.
5 *Unions* How do we interact with unions in order to:	
Improve relations Gain commitment Build skills Help them cope with the changing power base	Improve communications Shop steward training in such areas as problem solving and decision making Enhance current influences of shop stewards Initiate a joint management-union working party to prepare proposals for a participatory system (see 2a) Proposals to be developed by September.
6 *People problems* How do we manage people issues that will emerge from the change process:	
(a) Feelings of insecurity	By good communications and

Problem	*Action needed*
	keeping employees informed and involved in the change process. To be achieved through workshops (See 4.)
(b) Reduced opportunities for advancement	This should be overcome by job redesign and enrichment. No action appropriate at present.
(c) Resistance to change	It takes time but pre-requisites are elimination of insecurity, good communication and training to give new skills. Process to begin with workshop (See 4.)
(d) People unable to perform in a more complex environment	The onus is on managers to plan the right people in the right jobs and to train people to adapt. Managers should feel responsible for re-deploying people into jobs where they do feel comfortable if a mistake has been made. Each manager to be given personal objectives in this area.
(e) Increased expectation of reward	This will be handled via the job evaluation process. (See 2d.)
(f) People displaced (now and in the future)	Personnel to develop proposals for policies on redundancy due to organisation change by December.
7 *Time management* How do management organise their day-to-day activities to ensure they allocate time to staff development and long-term planning?	By eliminating unnecessary tasks, delegating and installing a more appropriate appraisal and work planning system. Individual action plans for improved time management will be developed and incorporated in personal objectives.
8 *Changing roles* How do we manage the people issues that will result from: Changing manager roles Specialists moving into teams?	By good communications and keeping employees informed and involved in the change process. Process to begin with workshop (See 4.)

Problem	*Action needed*
9 *Informing employees* What information should be given to employees in order to gain their commitment and to facilitate the change process?	The maximum amount of information on matters that affect employees should be given. Medium to achieve this will be improved communications (See 2c) and workshop (See 4.)
10 *Measurement of achievement of objectives* How do we measure the degree to which organisation objectives have been achieved?	Measurement should be based on: 1 Cost effectiveness 2 Productivity 3 Improved quality 4 Improved industrial relations 5 New capital investment in the plant because of increased profitability. Headman to take responsibility for feedback on increased effectiveness.

Summary

The problems can be overcome. The changes can best be facilitated if we, as managers:

1 Consult and participate where appropriate.
2 Listen to others problems and spend time over people issues.
3 Concentrate on developing the knowledge and capacities of ourselves and our staff.
4 Actively communicate.
5 Develop the view throughout the whole organisation that we all have the same overall objectives.
6 Enhance the influence of unions and others who feel threatened.

Appendix 2
Management Principles Workshop

Introduction

An objective of the management principles workshop described in Chapter Six, was to develop a relevant and practical set of guidelines to which the management group felt committed. These guidelines were intended for the use of all organisation members to control and direct the programme of organisation development and change.

This Appendix presents the guidelines developed by company X's management group. Plans developed by managers and supervisors during the implementation of the organisation development programme were evaluated against these guidelines.

Key guidelines

The following guidelines should be considered *key*: to be followed at all times.

1 The change process should take place at a pace that allows for the growing understanding of, and commitment towards, the change process by all employees.

2 The change process should reflect the history, current characteristics and future tasks of the company. Examples of changes that have taken place elsewhere should be seen as useful sources of ideas, not models to be followed.

3 Any change must be justified in terms of quality, productivity, cost and/or flexibility and not made for the sole reason of making changes.
4 The process or organisation improvement is relevant to all parts of the organisation.

Other guidelines

The following guidelines should be taken into consideration when planning the new organisation, and should be followed when they are relevant and appropriate.

Decision making

Decision making should be vested in the work group by:

1 Asking work group members to identify and propose solutions to their own day-to-day problems.
2 Listening to the solutions they generate.
3 Implementing promptly those solutions where possible.
4 Providing group recognition for effective problem solving.

Security

The organisation changes will generate feeling of insecurity amongst some employees. These feelings should be managed by:

1 Keeping people informed.
2 Introducing changes at a pace that reflects people's increasing understanding.
3 Eliminating feelings of insecurity relevant to:
   (*a*) Job redesign
   (*b*) Introduction of new technology.
4 Sound communication.
5 Involving people.
6 Listening to concerns and acting upon them.

Involvement

The more people are involved, the greater will be their understanding and commitment. Involvement can be achieved by:

1 Inviting people to participate in the development of plans, if this is practical.
2 Consulting with them on the plans, and being willing to change plans to reflect their views, but where this is impractical –

3 Informing people, listening to their concerns, and where possible acting to allay them.
4 Encouraging all employees to participate in planning their day-to-day work environment.

Learning and training

The change process can only be successful if people understand the process. Management must be prepared to identify training needs and support training programmes, where necessary contributing towards training activities themselves.

Job redesign

All departments should review the way work is currently organised to identify areas for improvement using the following principles:

1 Changes should be planned with and through the people involved.
2 Changes should be implemented in areas that are suitable and ready.
3 Initially, where changes involve a radical review of current practices, they should be done in an experimental, protected environment.
4 A step-by-step approach should be used.
5 Changes should be introduced against specific and measured targets.
6 Other interested parties, e.g. unions, interacting departments should be consulted.
7 With low risk: initial projects must be successful and accepted.
8 Accompanied by a major training effort.
9 New jobs should be multi-skilled and/or flexible. This will be a long-term objective for shopfloor jobs but in the short term opportunities should be taken to maximise flexibility within the skilled boundaries.
10 Both the nature of the technology and needs of the people should be taken into account.
11 Principles of job rotation and enrichment should be incorporated.

Autonomy

Work groups should be given maximum autonomy over decisions about day-to-day work organisation, e.g. task allocation, control over pace, breaks, relief, quality. But the degree of autonomy must be dependent on the achievement of clearly defined goals.

Role of specialists

Whilst recognising there is a need for specialist skills within the organisation and a requirement to maintain a balance of experience within business units, specialists should:

1 Take on a wider variety of jobs to increase width of skills, and therefore, flexibility.
2 Be more closely associated with production tasks to increase team spirit and focus the effort of specialists on shop floor problems.
3 Be rotated to increase skills and flexibility.

Communication

Change process must be associated with effective two-way communication to all employees. This requires:

1 Improving the system of communication.
2 Monitoring effectiveness of the new system.
3 Improving the content of the communication.
4 Training and people.
5 Being willing to share information with staff at all levels.

Supervision

Changes in work group practices will have a major impact on the role of the supervisor. The supervision must play a central role in ensuring the success of change programme. Therefore, any changes must be accompanied by:

1 Commitments on job security.
2 Involvement, consultation, information.
3 Associated training/workshop activities and particularly training in: running briefing meetings, running line meetings, nature of job redesign, reasons for organisation change, nature of organisation change.
4 An experimental approach, and in areas where the people are ready and the organisation suitable.

Unions

Changes in work group practices require union acceptance, therefore we should:

1 Involve union representatives in the development of any job design programme within their area.
2 Have training/workshop activities to meet union demand.

Appendix 3
Supervisor Workshop

Introduction

Following a series of management workshops the process of developing commitment to, and understanding of, the organisation development programme should 'cascade down' to the next level. In our case study the next level down was junior management or supervision.

This Appendix presents an example of the sort of material that is developed at a supervisor workshop. It is based on the workshop that took place in company X which was described in Chapter Seven. During this workshop the supervisors were asked to define what action they felt was needed to ensure progress of the organisation development programme by each of three groups; senior management; middle (department) management; and themselves.

The senior management agreed that they would:

1 Review these action proposals.
2 Decide on what action they (the senior management) should take in the light of the action proposals.
3 Review these action decisions with middle management.
4 Communicate these action decisions to the supervisors.

This Appendix lists the action items developed by the supervisors at the workshop in company X. In a typical supervisor workshop programme decisions to implement action on the items listed in parts 2 and 3 would be taken in department meetings.

Action to be taken by senior management

1 *Action item*

Provide security by developing long term investment plans for the organisation.

Response
Decisions on investment within the corporation are taken at the very highest levels. These decisions will take account of a variety of relevant influences, and one of these will be the historical plant performance. Senior management will continue to work with employees at all levels to ensure that standards of efficiency and flexibility make investment in the future attractive. This can only be achieved by continuing the process of steadily improving productivity through organisation development and the introduction of new technology.

2 *Action item*

Communicate long-term strategies and prospects of all employees.

Response
Communications will be prepared for monthly briefing groups as and when information is available.

3 *Action item*

Issue a statement guaranteeing that there will be no redundancy as a result of the organisation development programme.

Response
No employee will be made redundant as a direct result of changes taking place as part of the organisation development programme. Employment levels will however, need to be continuously reviewed in the light of any changes in the business situation, or the introduction of new technology.

4 *Action item*

Work with the unions to:

1 Reduce or eliminate demarcation.
2 Increase knowledge of the organistion development programme.
3 Ensure that the industrial relations climate is one in which progress can be made towards a more effective organisation.

Response
Management have invited the unions to join them in workshops to begin the process of consultation.

5 *Action item*

Communicate to all employees the reasons for, and objectives of, the organisation development programme.

Response
A communication on the organisation development programme will be prepared and given by the senior manager. This communication will take place following the union workshop.

6 *Action item*

Arrange for revised job descriptions and review payment systems to ensure that payment is commensurate to the new responsibilities.

Response
It is acknowledged that the organisation development programme will lead to both different expectations and a need for new systems. The development of new systems are planned.

7 *Action item*

Continuously demonstrate their commitment to the change programme.

Response
Senior management, both at corporate and plant level believe that they are committed to the organisation development programme. They have already spent time reviewing what changes in management style are necessary and are committed to continued work in this area.

Management have developed principles which will guide them in their approach to organisation development in the future. They will be discussing these principles with the supervisors.

The supervisors are invited to feed back to senior management examples of where their behaviour is counter to the new philosophies.

8 *Action item*

Ensure that action taken in each department is coordinated.

Response
All employees must ensure that we learn from each other's mistakes and successes.

9 *Action plan*

Arrange for supervision to visit plants where there has been successful organisation change.

Response
Managers will be reviewing the training needs of their subordinates.

10 *Action plan*

Make public the planned contraction of supervisor positions.

Response
The organisation development programme is based on the principles that change takes place at the right speed, in the right place, at the right time, and where opportunities present themselves. There is no blueprint for the future, and certainly no firm view of how many supervisors there will be.

11 *Action item*

Consider abolishing the clocking-on system in order to gain trust.

Response
It is felt that abolishing the clocking-on system is not appropriate at present. All management systems will, however, be continuously reviewed in the light of progress being made in the organisation development programme.

Action to be taken by middle management

1 Work with supervision to plan the organisation development programme, in particular:
   (*a*) Provide guidelines;
   (*b*) Define objectives;
   (*c*) Clarify ideas;
   (*d*) Run pilot schemes;
   (*e*) Agree implementation plans;
   (*f*) Establish a realistic but flexible timetable.
2 Analyse supervisor's training needs, attend and support training programmes to include:
   (*a*) Supervisor skills;
   (*b*) Team building and group organisation;
   (*c*) Participation;
   (*d*) Retraining of supervision displaced by the organisation changes.
3 Improve the communications system so that:
   (*a*) Supervisors are kept informed;
   (*b*) Supervisors are able to keep their subordinates informed;
   (*c*) The supervisor is the channel for communication to their people;

(*d*) Everyone has the same information;
(*e*) Information is relevant and comprehensive.

4 Receive feedback from meetings of employees and listen to suggestions and criticism from employees.
5 Continuously demonstrate their own commitment.
6 Systematically measure progress made.
7 Review targets during the settling in period following change.
8 Ensure that facilities and money are available to support the change.

Action to be taken by supervisors

1 Show commitment to the change process by demonstrating conviction, enthusiasm and readiness for change.
2 Improve communications to all employees.
3 Begin the process of organisation change by:
(*a*) Delegating more; getting people to take on more;
(*b*) Taking on a more advisory, counselling role;
(*c*) Reducing the amount of direct supervision;
(*d*) Establishing work groups;
(*e*) Reviewing the way work is organised;
(*f*) Increasing operator flexibility;
(*g*) Getting to know the people better as individuals.
4 Listen to employees more so that:
(*a*) Full use can be made of their ideas;
(*b*) Shopfloor values and ideas can be communicated to management.
5 Identify and implement training programmes to develop employee understanding of the change process.
6 Learn from their own and their colleagues mistakes and successes.
7 Work more closely with union representatives, shopfloor and management in order to increase trust.
8 Define their own training needs.
9 Ask for and act upon feedback from subordinates on their own performance.
10 Ensure employees receive rewards appropriate to the new way of working.
11 Ensure that quality and productivity standards are maintained during the change programme.

Appendix 4
Specialist Workshop

Introduction

This Appendix presents an example of the sort of material that is developed at a specialist workshop. It is based on a specialist workshop which took place in company X and is described in Chapter Seven. It is therefore intended to be typical of a workshop involving engineers who are to work in support of manufacturing teams and whose jobs are to be widened (and therefore despecialised). Examples could be provided for any specialist group – accountants, production controllers, buyers, trainers, quality engineers. The sort of response would be the same and many of the concerns raised by the engineers in this example would be felt by other specialist groups in the same situation.

In our case history the workshop members were asked to review the advantages and disadvantages of the organisation development programme, to define their concerns and the problems to be overcome and to develop an action plan to manage these concerns and problems. This Appendix presents a summary of the material recorded in company X during a specialist workshop.

Advantages and disadvantages for the organisation development programme

Advantages

1 Each engineer will increase his job knowledge and skills.

2 The jobs will become broader, more interesting, and more relevant.
3 Working in teams will increase team spirit and commitment.
4 Upgrading may be possible with increased and wider responsibilities.
5 Work through and project completion will be improved.
6 Recruitment and development of staff will be facilitated.

Disadvantages

1 Extensive training will be required.
2 There will no longer be a large and powerful functional department to protect the interests and status of specialists.
3 Some senior specialist jobs will disappear which will reduce promotion opportunities.
4 Because their responsibilities will be wider, the more highly qualified and senior engineers will be given more lower skilled tasks, which will lead, over time, to a loss of collective expertise in key specialist areas.
5 Radical change will be uncomfortable for many engineers and will lead to unrest.
6 Junior engineers will no longer have the support of their more experienced and senior colleagues.
7 The opportunity to specialise in areas of interest or knowledge will be reduced.

Problems to be overcome

1 The isolation of engineers resulting from working in multifunctional teams rather than single function departments.
2 The reduced career opportunities for engineers brought about by the reduction in the number of engineering supervisors.
3 The need to increase the width of knowledge and skills of all engineers.
4 The need to change the working relationships with supervisors and operators: more consulting, less directing.
5 The unwillingness or inability of some engineers to adapt to the new ways of working.
6 The reduction in specialist expertise that goes with the widening of engineering roles.
7 The increased workload during training period.

Concerns

1 Changes will be made too rapidly, without adequate consultation or training.
2 New roles and duties are not fully clear to all the people.
3 The job evaluation system is not designed for the new working methods, and will produce grading anomalies.
4 Loss of mobility and flexibility will occur unless a programme of rotation is implemented.

Action plans

1 A project group to be formed to develop a training plan to facilitate the development of the skills and knowledge needed to operate the new working methods, and in particular:
   (*a*) To plan how engineers can learn skills from each other;
   (*b*) To work with training department to develop relevant courses.

   Responsibility: John Smith
   Report by: 31st July, 19. .
   to reconvened workshop

2 Recommendations to be made to the board that a small central engineering department is maintained in order to:
   (*a*) Accomplish the tasks that will still need to be done by specialists;
   (*b*) Provide a centre of expertise with whom the engineers working in teams can consult;
   (*c*) Plan individual development programmes;
   (*d*) Manage training and development programmes for all the engineers working in teams;

   Responsibility:
   Headman to prepare recommendations for board based on discussions at the workshop.

3 All engineers to be consulted before allocation of individuals to specific work groups and plans to be discussed at a further workshop before implementation. Every effort to be made to accommodate the needs of engineers who feel unable to work effectively in the new system.

   Responsibility: Headman.

4 A project group to be formed to work with personnel to identify any job description or job evaluation issues that may occur due to the changing job responsibilities, and to prepare recommendations for action to overcome these issues. This project group also to consider the impact of new working practices on promotion prospects.

Responsibility: Fred Brown
August 31st, 19. . to reconvened workshop.

5 A further workshop to be held in order to:
(*a*) Discuss the reports of the two project teams;
(*b*) Consult with all the workshop members on the development of the plan;
(*c*) Provide more information with practical examples on the organisation development programme, and the reasons for it.

Appendix 5
Monthly Briefing Groups

Introduction

This proposed monthly briefing group system is designed to ensure effective communication in a 'role' organisation. This system might be unsuited to other types of organisations, and would need some adaptation to ensure that it meets the needs of any organisation that wishes to use a monthly briefing group system.

Objectives

1 To improve the quality and speed of communication between management and employees.
2 To improve levels of cooperation and trust between management and employees.

Terms of reference

1 The headman will be responsible for the preparation of monthly briefing notes.
2 The communications assistant will assist the headman with these responsibilities, and will also collect relevant information generated by other interested bodies (e.g. R & D, the joint consultative committee) for inclusion.

3 The briefing notes will be distributed and explained by the headman at a meeting with his managers.
4 Each manager will then hold a similar session with his subordinates, and this process will continue down the hierarchy until all employees have had the opportunity to attend a monthly briefing group. Through this process each department section or work team will form a monthly briefing group. The key requirement is that each individual has an opportunity to attend the same group each month. A monthly briefing group should comprise no more than 30 people.
5 Local material should be added to the briefing material as appropriate. The monthly briefing group chairman is responsible for the assembly of this additional material.
6 At each stage discussions of the briefing material should be encouraged.
7 Individuals may request additional information if their information needs cannot be met by the monthly briefing group chairman.
8 This additional information should be requested on a 'Request for information' form, which will define from whom the information is requested and how and when it should be provided (presented below).
9 Additional information may be provided:
   (*a*) In writing, by a named individual, within five working days; or
   (*b*) In writing, to the monthly briefing group chairman, one week before the next scheduled meeting; or
   (*c*) In person, at the next meeting.
10 All requests for information should be routed through the communications assistant who is responsible for any follow-up work and monitoring the effectiveness of the system.
11 A monthly briefing group which wishes to communicate information either upwards, or laterally, should do so in the form of a memo.

Chairmanship

Each manager or supervisor of a department, section or work team is responsible for scheduling and chairing the local monthly briefing group. He is also responsible for completing the 'Request for information' form shown overleaf.

Content

The briefing notes should normally contain:

1. Company, department and work team performance (output, sales, costs, quality, profits etc.).
2. Company, department, work team changes (conditions, benefits, appointments, structures etc.).
3. Company, department, work team plans (manpower, marketing, operations, finance etc.).
4. Employee relations issues (recent agreements, progress of negotiations etc.).
5. Any other significant events or management decisions and the reasons for them. But should exclude:
   (*a*) Items that could affect commercial security;
   (*b*) Topics whose inclusion would be contrary to the conventions of industrial relations procedures.

MONTHLY BRIEFING GROUPS
REQUEST FOR INFORMATION

Monthly briefing group:

Date held:

Person responsible:

Request for information made to:

Nature of request:

Response requested (delete as appropriate)

1. In writing to . . . . within 5 working days of the date below.

2. In writing to the undersigned, by one week before the next monthly briefing group meeting due to be held on . . . .

3. By a presentation at the next monthly briefing group meeting to be held on . . . .

Signed: . . . .
Date: . . . .

This completed form should be forwarded to the Communications Assistant.

Appendix 6 Management—Union Workshops

In unionised organisations the union (or unions) must be involved in organisation change. This involvement should be begun with a management-union workshop, which should take place after the workshops for management and supervisors, but before any systematic work with unionised employees. This Appendix presents an example of the sort of material that is developed at a workshop, attended by both management and union representatives. The workshop is designed to increase union representatives' understanding of the organisation development programme and to increase their readiness to support change. It is based on the workshop that took place in company X which is described in Chapter Nine. During this workshop, union representatives were asked to define their concerns with the organisation development programme. In addition both union and management were asked to define what action was needed (a) by management and (b) by the union, to support the change programmes. Because management and unions developed presentations with similar content, they are summarised in this appendix as one set of action ideas.

Organisation issues, problems and concerns

1 *Job security*: Employees in company X were worried about their future security. There was consensus that the organisation development programme would be facilitated if security needs were met. Discussion of this problem focused on three areas:

(*a*) Redundancy due to drop in orderboard or the introduction of new technology may be inevitable. The union believes the company should be taking active steps to minimise the effect of such redundancy on their members. Examples of effective policies in other organisations should be looked at e.g. British Steel, Italian car industry. The company should consult with the union whilst developing these policies.

(*b*) The company should not expect the union to actively support job redesign activities that will lead to the redundancy of union members. The company should be willing to offer guarantees of job security for any employees who become actively involved in the organisation development programme.

(*c*) The union are being asked to cooperate in changing company X towards a more Japanese organisation. The Japanese achieve high levels of productivity, but also offer job security. The union believe the two go together.

2 *Speed of change*: The changes proposed by management will take a long time to implement. Management should avoid generating hostility through premature action.

3 *Quality*: Achieving high quality must be given greater priority. Currently management and supervision are seen to emphasise meeting short-term production targets rather than long-term improvements through higher quality.

4 *Involvement and consultation*: Currently suggestions being put forward by shopfloor employees are being ineffectively handled. The main problems that occur were identified as follows:

(*a*) The process of decision making is elevated to too high a level: the decision makers do not understand the problem;
(*b*) Suggestions that are made do not result in action;
(*c*) When action does take place, the shopfloor is not informed;
(*d*) Credit for effective action following shopfloor suggestions is being given to specialists.

Suggestions from the shopfloor are also not encouraged. Management prefer to deal with problems by either bringing in specialists, or appointing extra supervision. The operators, who understand the problem, are often not consulted.

5 *Management style*: Improvements need to be made in the way union members are managed, and in particular:

(*a*) Supervisors need to be given more authority so that they do not need to pass problems upwards;
(*b*) The shopfloor should be treated with more courtesy;
(*c*) Shopfloor ideas and suggestions should be listened to more effectively;

(*d*) All employees should be treated equally to get rid of the 'us *v* them' attitudes;
(*e*) The welfare of individual employees who fall on bad times should be a greater management concern.

6 *Open and honest communications*: There is a need to improve the openness and honesty of communications between all employees: management, supervision, staff, shopfloor. An improved system should be developed that incorporates:
(*a*) More information;
(*b*) Two-way information;
(*c*) Sensitive handling of confidential information.

7 *Training*: The system of training should be reviewed if organisation development principles are to be introduced. Particular concerns were:
(*a*) Flexibility requires a major training programme to build skills;
(*b*) The company should be seen to be supporting training by allocating resources;
(*c*) Shopfloor training has not been seen as effective in the past.

An effective training programme that provided operators with the necessary knowledge and skills will develop confidence and trust between the shopfloor and management.

8 *Rewards*: There is an expectation that involvement in job redesign will be financially rewarded. Significant changes will generate a need for a revised reward system.

9 *Corporate strategies*: We are being told that company X must become the lowest cost producer in order to ensure all our futures, but we may achieve greater profitability through organisation development and see the profit being utilised elsewhere in the corporation. Company X would then still have no future.

What management should do

1 Take active steps to deal with the problems and concerns identified at the workshop.

2 Spend time and effort on further discussions on the organisation development programme with union representatives to:
(*a*) Keep them informed;
(*b*) Develop their understanding.

3 Keep the union informed on planned new technology and other policy decisions that affect union members.

4 Be sensitive to the conflict for representatives in joint-planning. They may be seen to be endorsing management plans that are perceived as harmful to some members.
5 Invest more in machinery.
6 Prepare and implement a training programme for union members so that they can understand the organisation development process.
7 Be aware that the union district committee will have to be consulted and may not initially support the process.
8 Consult with unions on the introduction of trial schemes under a sheltered agreement.
9 Ensure that people's skills are fully utilised.

What the union should do

1 Support the introduction of organisation development.
2 Support management in their action plan to deal with the problems and concerns identified at the workshop.
3 Establish with management a framework to discuss future changes to achieve:
   (*a*) Understanding;
   (*b*) Consultation;
   (*c*) Action.
4 Consult with management on the introduction of trial schemes under a sheltered agreement.
5 Support a training programme for union members so that they can understand the organisation development programme.
6 Differentiate between day-to-day problems and the achievements of long-term objectives when considering their approach towards issues. This involves adopting a joint problem solving approach before adopting traditional bargaining roles. It will also be necessary for the union to evaluate how they will have to change in order to operate in a changing role.

Conclusions

Both management and the union agreed that the organisation development programme represented an effective way of increasing flexibility and productivity. Both agreed that they should be searching for ways in which they could work together to ensure continued employment at company X for the benefit of all employees.

Reading List

Chapter One

Emery, F.E., *Systems Thinking*, 1969, Penguin

Provides a practical guide to using a systems approach to manage organisational change.

Handy, C.B., *Understanding Organisations*, 1976, Penguin

A popular and highly readable book that provides a brief yet comprehensive overview of ideas and techniques in many aspects of organisations: motivation, leadership, power, group workings, culture and politics. Handy is concerned with how basic concepts can be applied to different organisation problems.

Hausser, D.L., Pecorella, P.A. and Wissler, A.L., *Survey Guided Development*, 1977, University Associates

Practical guide to diagnosing an organisation culture, and providing data that can be used to develop missions and plans for the future.

Jayarem, G.K., 'Open Systems Planning' in Bennis, Benne, Chin and Corey (eds) *The Planning of Change*, 1976, Holt, Rinehart & Winston

An important practical paper in a useful book of readings.

Katz, D. and Kahn, L.K., *The Social Psychology of Organisation*, 1978, Wiley

One of the best reviews of the field of organisational and industrial psychology, with emphasis on the system approach and the link between the organisation and its environment.

Lawrence, P.R. and Lorsh, J.W., *Organisation and Environment*, 1967, Harvard

A classic book that should be read by anyone seriously interested in the design of organisations, both for their detailed findings and for their conclusions that different ways of designing organisations can be equally effective, depending on the circumstances.

Woodcock, M. and Francis, D., *Organisation Development through Teambuilding*, 1981, Gower

This book looks at the benefits and dangers of teambuilding as an organisation development strategy.

Chapter Two

Adair, J., *Effective Leadership: a Self-Development Manual*, 1983, Gower

Anthony, W.P., *Participative Management*, 1978, Addison-Wesley

Suggests how managers can become more responsive and effective by using participatory approaches to achieving organisational goals.

Etzioni, A., 'Organisation Control Structures' in March, J.G. (ed), *Handbook of Organisations*, 1965, Rand McNally.

Reviews how social control can be maintained through commitment to organisation values from the industrial sociological perspective.

Guest, D. and Knight, K. (eds), *Putting Participation into Practice*, 1979, Gower

Contains detailed case histories of the various approaches to a more participative mode of decision making and operating at the workplace.

Hebdon, J. and Shaw, G., *Pathways to Participation*, 1977, Assoc. Bus. Progs. Ltd.

Describes a number of schemes in different organisations, each designed to provide for a growing demand for greater influence on decisions over their working lives from an increasingly educated workforce. Emphasis is placed on the process of managing the introduction of change.

IPM, *Practical Participation and Involvement, Vol. 3, The Individual and the Job*, 1982

Describes and illustrates, with case histories, action to increase employee involvement through job design, Quality Circles, attitude surveys, appraisals and suggestion schemes.

Vroom, V.H. and Yetton, P.W., *Leadership and Decision Making*, 1973, University of Pittsburgh Press

Examines when managers should use authoritative, when consultative and when participatory approaches to decision making: provides a number of case histories to illustrate the way managers vary their behaviour with the demands of the situation.

Chapter Three

Benedict, R., *The Chrysanthemum and the Sword*, 1967, Routledge and Kegan Paul

Reviews and compares social attitudes in Japan and Britain.

Braid, J., 'Japanese Cultures in Co. Durham', *Personnel*, Mar., 1982

A series of articles covering values, structures, cultures and attitudes within Japanese manufacturing companies, and their relevance for the West.

Dore, R., *British Factory – Japanese Factory*, 1973, University of California Press

A fascinating comparison of the experience of working in large manufacturing plants in two cultures.

Hauser, M., 'Are Japanese Workaholics?' *Personnel*, Dec., 1981

Lambert, P., 'Selecting Japanese Management Practices for Import', *Personnel*, Jan., 1982

Ouchi, W.G., *Theory Z: How American Business can meet the Japanese Challenge*, 1981, Addison-Wesley

This widely acclaimed book ascribes the secret of Japan's business success to a unique style of management which combines long range planning, consensus decision making and building strong employee commitment.

Teasdale, A., 'The Paradoxes of Japanese Success', *Personnel*, Nov., 1981

Thurley, K., 'The Japanese Model: Practical Reservations and Surprising Opportunities', *Personnel*, Feb., 1982

Chapter Four

Child, J., *Organisation: a Guide to Problems and Practice*, 1977, Harper & Row

A highly readable introduction to the field of organisation design written for practical managers as well as those engaged in study: excellent section on hierarchy and span of control.

Davis, S. and Lawrence, P., *Matrix Organisations*, 1977, Addison-Wesley

Reviews organisation designs that allow a focus on task completion whilst maintaining the advantages of function integration.

Galbraith, J., *Designing Complex Organisations*, 1973, Addison-Wesley

Deals with more unconventional approaches to designing organisations in order to encourage team work and task completion: a theoretical book.

Handy, C.B., *Op cit*., Chapter 1

Legge, K. and Mumford, E. (eds), *Designing Organisations for Satisfaction and Efficiency*, 1978, Gower

Collection of articles originally published in *Personnel Review*. Examination of the effect of job satisfaction, or the lack of it, on individual job performances. The link between individual job performance and organisational performance is then explored.

Chapter Five

Beckhard, R. and Reuben, T.H., *Organisation Transitions*, 1977, Addison-Wesley

Offers specific help for organisation leaders coping with planning for the future and overviewing the transitions, whilst simultaneously managing current work.

Davis, N.L. and McCallon, E., *Workshop*, 1974, Learning Concepts

Relates the workshop concept to the adult learning process and presents an unpretentious overview of a practical framework for planning learning events: does not specifically relate workshops to organisation development programmes.

Marquiles, N. and Wallace, J., *Organisation Change: Techniques and Applications*, 1973, Scott Freeman

Practical description of techniques to manage organisation change to ensure that it is smooth and effective.

Vroom and Yetton, *op cit*., Chapter 2

Chapter Seven

Aldag, R.J. and Brief, A.P., *Task Design and Employee Motivation*, 1979, Scott Freeman

Relates job design to individual motivation and the changing role of the worker in western society.

Bailey, J., *Job Redesign and Work Organisation*, 1983, Prentice-Hall

An excellent, up-to-date and practical overview of the field.

Birchall, D., *Job Redesign*, 1975, Gower

A planning and implementation guide for managers.

Hackman, J.R. and Oldham, G.R., *Work Redesign*, 1980, Addison-Wesley

A comprehensive and clearly written analysis of the benefits to both the individual and organisation of work redesign, and of how the transition to new ways of working can be managed.

Handy, C.B., *op cit*., Chapter 1

Hill, P., *Towards a New Philosophy of Management*, 1971, Gower

An account of the introduction of autonomous group in Shell UK, plus a review of the literature.

Klein, L., *New Forms of Work Organisation*, 1976, Cambridge University Press

A straightforward brief introduction to autonomous work groups.

Mohr, W.L., *Quality Circles: a Practical Guide*, 1982, Gower

Written for both professional and general reader, this book explores the way quality circle concepts can be introduced, and the way quality circles lead to more knowledgeable, motivated and satisfied employees.

Chapter Eight

Batten, J., *Expectations and Possibilities*, 1981, Addison-Wesley

A comprehensive and direct review of a style of management based on clearly expressed expectations; contains practical techniques for using this approach.

Brown, L.D., *Managing Conflict at Organisational Interfaces*, 1982, Addison-Wesley

Describes a simple conceptual framework for analysing and managing different conflict situations.

Handy, *op. cit*., Chapter 1

Hart, L.B., *Learning from Conflict*, 1981, Addison-Wesley

Provides suggestions for activities to help turn conflict into productive force.

Jayarem, *op. cit*., Chapter 1

Katz and Kahn, *op. cit*., Chapter 1

Chapter Nine

Scott Myers, M., *Managing without Unions*, 1976, Addison-Wesley. *Managing with Unions*, 1978, Addison-Wesley

Companion volumes which review the relationships between styles of management and patterns of union-management cooperation.

Chapter Ten

Bailey, *op. cit.*, Chapter 7
Davis and Lawrence, *op. cit.*, Chapter 4
Handy, *op. cit.*, Chapter 1
Klein, *op. cit.*, Chapter 7
Schein, E.H. and Bennis, W.G., *Personal–Organisational Change through Group Methods*, 1965, Wiley

An overall description of a range of training and group development techniques: theoretically based in group dynamics school.

Ulshak, F., Nathanson, L. and Gillan, P., *Small Group Problem Solving*, 1981, Addison-Wesley

Describes the way small groups operate to solve problems and ways of making group operations more effective and efficient.

Vroom, V.H. and Deci, E.L. (eds), *Management and Motivation*, 1970, Penguin

Invaluable collection of the principal source material on style of leadership, motivation of groups, and performance, productivity and morale.

Woodcock, M., *Team Development Manual*, 1979, Gower

Contains practical exercises to improve team working: brainstorming, force field analysis, openness, listening, counselling, and many more.

Chapter Eleven

Garnett, J., *The Manager's Responsibility for Communication*, 1980, Industrial Society

Reviews the significance of effective communication and how it can be achieved.

IPM, *Practical Participation and Involvement: Vol. 1, Communication in Practice*, 1981

Describes, with examples, communications practices in different organisations.

Reeves, T.K. and Harper, D., *Surveys at Work*, 1981, McGraw-Hill

Provides guidelines on how to manage upward communications through surveys, and discusses the problems and pitfalls.

Chapter Twelve

Davis and McCallon, *op. cit.*, Chapter 5

IPM, *Practical Participation and Involvement: Vol. 4, Meeting Education and Training Needs*, 1982

Provides guidance and information on education and training activities devoted to promoting employee involvement: there is an emphasis on learning as a continuous element in a developing organisation.

Schein, E.H., *Process Consultancy*, 1969, Addison-Wesley

A sound discussion of group processes and procedures and the way that they can be facilitated by effective consulting methods. Also contains a short history of group theory.

Varney, G.H., *Organisation Development for Managers*, 1977, Addison-Wesley

Examines all facets of OD in a practical, do-it-yourself way, and explains how to recognise the need for change, collect the relevant data, and plan the change process.

Woodcock, M., *op. cit.*, Chapter 10

Chapter Thirteen

Ritzer, G. and Trice, H.M., *Occupation in Conflict: a study of the Personnel Manager*, 1969, Cornell University

One of the few studies that looks at the conflict that almost always seems to accompany the role of the personnel manager.

Index

Adair, J. 197
adult learning 71, 150
Aldag, R.S. 199
Anthony, W.P. 197
appraisal system 99, 171
Argyris, C. 71
attitude change 71
autonomous work group 39, 44, 80, 126-9, 130, 138, 161, 166, 177

Bailey, J. 200, 201
Batten, J. 200
Beckhard, R. 199
Benedict, R. 29-30, 198
Bennis, W.G. 201
Birchall, D. 200
Blake, R.R. 39
Braid, J. 198
Brief, A.P. 199
briefing groups 142, 146-7, 188-91
Brown, L.D. 200
building relationships:
  boss-subordinate 106-8
  inter-group 101-6, 133
business structures 52-5, 129-33

Child, J. 48, 198
communications 29, 44, 48-9, 52, 63, 112-13, 140-54, 166, 171, 173, 178-80, 188-91, 194
Communication:
  principles of 149-52
Company X:
  description 44-5
consensus decision making 27, 31, 38
consultancy support 155-7
career growth 38
cost reduction 23
counselling 136
creative thinking 103-4

Davis, N.L. 199, 202
Davis, S. 199, 201

Deci, E.L. 201
decision making and involvement 17-20, 65-6, 76, 78
delegatory management style 47-8
Dore, R. 198
Drucker, P. 39

Emery, F.E. 196
employment conditions 25
environmental trends 14
Etzioni, A. 197
expectation analysis 104-7

Francis, D. 197
functional integration 47-51

Galbraith, J. 199
Garnett, J. 201
Gillan, P. 201
Guest, D. 197

Hackman, J.R. 200
Handy, C.B. 9-15, 51, 101, 196, 199, 200, 201
Harper, D. 202
Hart, L.B. 200
Hauser, M. 198
Hausser, D.L. 196
headman: definition 58
role 74-7
Hebdon, J. 197
Herzberg, F. 39
hierarchy 47-50, 162
Hill, P. 200
hostility management 67-8, 91-2

induction 26
Industrial Society, The 142
information needs 69-70
interviewing skills 146
IPM 197, 202

Japan:
car industry 20
economic growth 20, 117
Japanese manufacturing organisation:
capital employed 22
communications 29, 140-3
consensus decision making 27, 31
cost reduction 23
employment conditions 25
finance 24
induction 26
management of change 31
management style 25-7, 80
Quality Circles 28-9, 33-6
quality performance 21-2
recruitment 26
supervisor role 27-8
suggestion schemes 23, 29
suppliers 25
teamwork 21, 27-32, 38-9
training 26
transferability to West 32-3
union relations 31, 193
use of technology 24-7
welfare 25
Jayarem, G.K. 196, 200
job evaluation 39, 121, 160-4, 171, 186-7
job redesign 44, 80, 93, 96-7, 121, 161, 166, 177, 193
job rotation 39, 80, 93
job security 117, 176, 192

Kahn, L.K. 196
Katz, D. 196
Kleen, L. 200, 201
Knight, K. 197

Lambert, P. 198
Lawrence, P. 199, 201
Lawrence, P.R. 7, 197
Legge, K. 199

listening skills 68-9
Lorsh, J.W. 7, 197

management principles 65-75, 78, 115, 126
manpower planning 131
Marquiles, N. 199
matrix management 52, 127, 130-3
McCallon, E. 199, 202
McGregor, D. 39
measurement of change 63, 174
Mohr, W.L. 200
Mumford, E. 199

Nathanson, L. 201
new technology agreement 193

Oldham, G.R. 200
open systems 8, 100, 103-4
operator:
  definition 85
  workshop 93-7
Opinion Research Centre 140
organisation audit 98-101, 104
organisation cultures
  origins 11-14
  person 11-14
  power 9-14, 66
  role 10-14, 56, 101, 133, 160-1
  task 10-14, 142
organisations:
  diversity of 6-7
organisation measurement 155
organisation structures
  business structures 52-5, 129-33
  functional integration 47-51
  hierarchy 47-50, 162
  matrix management 52
  span of control 48-50
  team development 126-39
Ouchi, W.G. 3, 38, 198
Owen, R. 39

payment systems 6, 25, 44, 161, 171, 181
Pecorella, P.A. 196
person culture 11-14
personnel systems 62, 160-4
planning workshop 58-65, 115
power culture 9-14, 66
presentation skills 149
problem solving approach 34, 54, 72-3, 144-50

Quality Circles 28, 29, 33-6, 44, 93, 96
quality performance 21-2, 38, 193
questionnaire design 146

recruitment 26
redundancy 180, 182, 193
Reeves, T.K. 202
Reuben, T.H. 199
Ritzer, C. 202
role analysis 104, 107
role culture 10-14, 56, 101, 133, 160-1

salary systems *see* payment systems
Schein, G.H. 201-2
Scott-Myers, M. 201
Shaw, G. 197
socio-technical approach 39
span of control 48-50
specialists: definition 85
specialist workshops 85, 89-93, 184-7
succession planning 131
suggestion schemes 23, 29
supervisor: definition 85
supervisor role 27-8, 133-8

supervisor workshop 86-9, 179-83
suppliers 25
survey techniques 146

task culture 10-14, 142
teamwork 27-32, 38-9, 47, 72-3, 126-9, 161
Teasdale, A. 198
theory Z 3, 38, 44
Thurley, K. 198
time management 173
trade union 31, 39, 63, 94-5, 109-25, 143, 170-1, 178-80, 192-5
training and development 26, 44, 62, 118, 122, 130-2, 149, 151, 154, 157-9, 171, 177, 182-3, 186, 194
Trice, H.M. 202

Ulshak, F. 201
union *see* trade union

Varney, G.H. 202
Vroom, V.H. 198, 199, 201

Wallace, J. 199
welfare 25
Wissler, A.L. 196
Woodcock, M. 197, 201, 202
worker director 16, 44
worker participation 16-19, 171
workshop approach 39, 56-8, 75-7
workshop principles 65-74
workshop: types
  boss-subordinate 106-8
  building inter-group co-operation 101-6, 133
  management planning 58-65, 115
  management principles 65-75, 78, 115, 126, 162
  management–union 114-24
  operator 85, 93-7
  organisation audit 98-101, 104
  specialist 85, 89-93, 162-3, 184-7
  supervisor 85-9, 173-83

Yetton, P.W. 198, 199